The Zen of Business

The Zen of Business

ANCIENT WISDOM TO HELP MODERN LEADERS LEAD WITH INTENTION, CLARITY, AND PURPOSE

KEITH EDWARD ROBERTS III

WILEY

Library of Congress Cataloging-in-Publication Data is Available:

ISBN 9781394309962 (Cloth)
ISBN 9781394309986 (ePDF)
ISBN 9781394309979 (ePub)

Cover Design: Wiley
Cover Image: © chekat/Getty Images
Author Photo by Andrea Flanagan

SKY10100188_031825

For my sons, Gavin and Quinn.
This book is to show you it's possible
to live beyond your wildest
dreams while making the world
a better place.

Contents

Foreword   *ix*

Preface   *xi*

Introduction: Becoming Zenman   1

Part 1   Begin   11

Chapter 1   Shoshin   13

Chapter 2   The Four Noble Truths   17

Chapter 3   Finding Your Way   39

Chapter 4   The Noble Eightfold Path   51

Part 2   Wisdom (*panna*)   61

Chapter 5   Right Understanding   63

Chapter 6   Impermanence   75

Chapter 7   Wabi-Sabi (侘び寂び)   83

Chapter 8   Right Thought   91

Chapter 9   Being Present (Sati)   101

Part 3   Morality (*sila*)   111

Chapter 10   Right Speech   113

Chapter 11   Zen and the Art of Communication   123

Chapter 12   Right Action   133

Chapter 13   Embracing Your Inner Monk   143

Chapter 14   Forest Bathing (Shinrin Yoku)   151

Chapter 15   Right Livelihood   157

Chapter 16   Ikigai   163

Chapter 17   Vision, Mission, and Values   173

Part 4   Mind (*samadhi*)   181

Chapter 18   Right Effort   183

Chapter 19   Misogi   191

Chapter 20   Right Mindfulness   199

Chapter 21   The Law of Attraction   207

Chapter 22   Right Concentration   213

Chapter 23   The Enlightened Entrepreneur   219

Acknowledgments   227

About the Author   229

Index   *231*

Foreword

In today's fast-paced, hustle-driven business world, finding balance can feel like an impossible task. Many entrepreneurs and leaders chase success at the cost of their peace, relationships, and sometimes even their health. But what if success didn't have to come with sacrifice? What if there was a way to build thriving businesses while cultivating inner calm, personal growth, and a positive impact on the world? This book offers a path to that balance.

The Zen of Business is a timely guide for modern leaders looking to align their entrepreneurial ambitions with ancient principles that transcend the noise of current trends. In a world obsessed with quick fixes and surface-level solutions, this book digs deeper, providing readers with a tool kit grounded in Buddhist and Eastern philosophies that have stood the test of time.

The author, whom I deeply respect and admire, has a unique ability to bridge ancient wisdom with modern business acumen. His perspective isn't just insightful—it's necessary. He offers readers more than just business advice; he offers a philosophy for life, one that is rooted in mindfulness, compassion, and the recognition that true success is not just about what you achieve but how you achieve it.

Whether you are a seasoned entrepreneur, a leader navigating complex challenges, or someone simply looking for a better way to balance work and life, *The Zen of Business* will provide you with the tools to create lasting success in a way that honors both yourself and the people you lead.

I hope you find the same depth of wisdom and inspiration in reading this book as I have in my friendship with its author. His unique perspective, shaped by years of study and personal experience, is a gift to anyone seeking not just success but fulfillment.

This is not just a book on business; it's a road map for living with purpose, integrity, and impact.

—Bennie Fowler, Denver Broncos,
Super Bowl 50 Champions

Preface

It is absolutely possible to be a successful entrepreneur or business leader in a way that is positive for your karma, your employees, and the world. I wrote this book to help align core Buddhist and ancient Eastern wisdom into a toolbox for modern leaders. In today's hustle-preneur culture, it's easy to get lost in the hype of passing trends. Yes, a cold plunge is going to reduce inflammation and increase blood flow and overall cardiovascular health, but it's not a guarantee to make your business successful.

Rather than embrace the fad trending on social media this week, I want to provide you with a toolbox of ancient practices that modern science has proven to have profound benefits. When applied to business, these techniques produce exponential results in culture, productivity, innovation, and profits.

You do not need to embrace Buddhism to benefit from the following lessons. These truths are for anyone to understand. The practices can be adopted and applied regardless of the reader's spiritual beliefs.

Life is too short to learn everything through experience. I hope that this book helps you avoid some of the potholes I stepped into and empowers you to capitalize on the opportunities you encounter.

Introduction:
Becoming Zenman

From my first memories, I struggled with religion. I grew up in a tiny town in rural Indiana. When I was five years old, my father's cousin convinced my parents to have me accompany them to their church, followed by Sunday school. The church service didn't stick in my mind, but Sunday school did. The adult was telling the story of Adam and Eve's experience in the Garden of Eden to my class. As a curious child who was consumed with dinosaurs, I persisted in asking a series of questions that annoyed the parent leading the group. What had happened to the Mesozoic era in this story?

Eventually, she had me sit in the corner for the remainder of Sunday school. That was my last time being invited to join my relatives for church. I hadn't intended to be disruptive or disrespectful in any way. It was genuine curiosity. Even at the early age of five, I had seen dinosaur bones at the La Brea Tar Pits when we made the Griswold Family road trip to Disneyland that was a rite of passage for Gen X. The proof existed right there in the middle of LA. Dinosaurs are real, and I guess even at an early age, I was a fan of debating different ideas and beliefs.

Fast forward a decade to advanced biology class during my freshman year in high school, which reinforced my questioning of the beliefs most of my peers embraced. I distinctly remember sitting next to my friend Mike—with whom I had played soccer for most of my life—just closing his book when we got to the chapter on evolution. Shutting the book meant he shut his mind to any ideas that differed or challenged the belief he was born into. I always struggled with the thought "What if I was born in the wrong place?"

Everywhere else in the world, billions of different people have the same devotion to their religion. Christians, Muslims, Jews, Hindus, and followers of every other belief firmly believe that the "others" are wrong and will suffer eternal damnation or whatever retribution their dogma dictates. As a little boy, this tormented me. I did not want to make the wrong choice when it came to something as crucial as my eternal being. Coupled with the learnings of evolution, this shaped me into a devout atheist. At that time, learning about evolution meant that I no longer had to find the right religion, and I embraced science. For the next four years, my belief was that of a devoted atheist with no need or desire for organized religion.

That was just the beginning of my journey.

Finding Entrepreneurship

The first time I remember hearing the word "entrepreneur" was two years before my evolution breakthrough in seventh-grade economics class. I clearly remember the teacher's definition of an entrepreneur as "someone who would face multiple failures in life before possibly reaching any success." He went on to expand on how it was a life of hardship that could lead to financial ruin and despair. In my day, the "safe" path was the corporate job; to be even more specific, I was meant to be an engineer. That was my introduction to the world of entrepreneurship, and rather than convincing me to take the safe path in life, it had the opposite effect. I knew right there that I was going to be an entrepreneur.

Ever since I was a boy, the best way to motivate me was to tell me I couldn't do something. That is one of the most common characteristics of founders. We see a challenge not as an obstacle but as an opportunity.

I remember a poster of Robert Frost's poem "The Road Less Traveled" hanging in my grandmother's bedroom. The final stanza has been burned into my subconscious.

Somewhere ages and ages hence:

Two roads diverged in a wood, and I—

I took the one less traveled by,

And that has made all the difference.

That stanza struck a chord in me that has resonated since, especially **"I took the one less traveled by, and that has made all the difference."** The idea of taking the road less traveled was only reinforced by my middle school economics teacher telling the class, "You can't build your own business—you will fail," which was all the motivation I needed. That 12-year-old kid decided then and there that I would own my first business before my 30th birthday.

That might sound like an audacious goal for many people, while for others it might appear conservative. For the contingent that feels the goal was too lofty, I would offer this perspective from Michelangelo: "The greatest danger for most of us is not that our aim is too high and we miss it, but that it is too low and we reach it." **Aim for your dreams, and even if you don't reach every goal, life will still be extraordinary.**

The other half who see starting their first business by the age of 30 as a conservative goal could have a skewed perspective by looking at Steve Jobs, who was 21 when he co-founded Apple with Steve Wozniak in his garage, or Larry Page and Sergey Brin, who started Google at the ripe old age of 24. Most successful startup founders are between 35 and 45 years old. Our society today focuses so intensely on the unicorns that most fail to see the significant number of failures.

Singles and doubles win ballgames. You have a much lower probability of success and are likelier to strike out if you swing for the fences every time you come up to bat.

The same is true in business. Consistent results create profitable businesses and companies that are better positioned for acquisition if that is the end goal. Don't misinterpret this as avoiding all risk or playing too safe in business and life. By all means, set lofty goals; just ensure they're plausible. It's better to make some progress than to strike out because you are trying to hit a grand slam or even worse because you need to. A couple of times in my business, I had to sell a job to make payroll, which was a horrible place to be and which I hope you never experience personally.

Not only is this a terrible mindset when entering a business negotiation, but it also decreases the probability of closing the sale. We have a saying in poker: **Scared money never wins.** Desperation is an unattractive quality both for a potential mate and in business dealings. Even at the energetic level, it's much better to come from an abundance mindset than a scarcity belief.

Finding My Path

My introduction to Buddhism came much later. Fast-forward to my first semester in college, and I met a man who would change my life forever. College for me was a small art school that specialized in photography and motion pictures called Brooks Institute in Santa Barbara, California. To be completely honest, it was heavenly. To this day, after being fortunate enough to travel all over the world, Santa Barbara is still hands down my favorite place on planet Earth.

The program at Brooks was intense but considered the best in the world. To pay for living in one of the most beautiful and hence expensive cities in the country, I worked six days a week as a bartender at night. This meant too many late nights with excessive alcohol consumption. Additionally, I smoked a pack or more of Camels a day—a stark contrast from the man who would change the course of my life for the better.

One of my classmates was a monk named Lopsang. He worked directly with the Dalai Lama, who sent him to the United States with the goal of attending a series of higher-education institutions. Lopsang was the first example that I was awake to of "when the student is ready, the teacher will appear."

Although Brooks was a melting pot of artists from all over the globe, Lopsang stood out among the class. Most of the students dressed like a grunge band from Seattle, and we had a solid contingent of expedition-ready photo-vest-wearing classmates, but Lopsang was the only one in saffron monk robes. During break I would grab whatever soda had the most caffeine in the vending machine and chain smoke two cigarettes. I used to light the second smoke from the cherry of the first while polluting my body with hapless disregard. After observing me for a few weeks, Lopsang started asking questions, like "Why do you prefer breathing cigarette smoke over the beautiful ocean air?" To which there really isn't an intelligent response. Instead of feeling like he was passing judgment, his questions made me contemplate the choices that had become unhealthy habits.

Our conversations deepened throughout the fall as Lopsang introduced me to concepts that intrigued rather than polarized me. The first was moderation. Buddha learned that excess isn't the path to Nirvana, just as self-deprivation isn't the path to enlightenment. As a chain-smoking bartender, my life was far from moderate. Although I didn't shift to Buddhism before Lopsang left for the next college, he was instrumental in helping me find my path. Before departing at the end of his time at Brooks, Lopsang shared ideas that lit a fire in me to shift from a life of excess to one of clarity and moderation.

Over the course of the next few years I dove deeper into Buddhism, eventually shifting from atheism to taking refuge in what are known as the three jewels: Buddha, Dharma, and Sangha. In the early '90s, it was a lot less common for a Westerner to completely embrace Buddhism than it is today. I can't tell you how many family holidays devolved into a heated debate because I didn't follow the traditional path of Christianity or, more importantly, "didn't believe in and fear God."

Combining the Business and the Spiritual

Over the past few decades, it's become mainstream and even hip to use "Zen" in marketing or the nomenclature of companies like Zendesk, Zenfolio, ZenPayroll, and Zenefits. At the time of this writing, there are 724 active trademarks containing the word "Zen" registered with the United States Patent and Trademark Office. That wasn't the case when I started my agency. I had been doing freelance creative work at night while grinding it out during the day at a mind-numbing, soul-sucking job designing reports for a market research firm. When the opportunity presented itself in the form of a severance package, I made the decision to start the business the seventh-grade version of myself had vowed to do before turning 30. At the time, I was 26. Since the entire company consisted of a Buddhist creative guy building websites under the stairs in his loft, the name was "Zenman."

The first year was lean, but I managed to make a little more than the corporate cubicle job paid. It consisted of any work that I could generate by rubbing two sticks together. It required becoming a salesperson, which is the opposite personality type from creatives, while simultaneously building a portfolio of work to show potential clients. In the early days, it was truly the Wild West of the web. Amazon was still losing money in 1998, a significant percentage of businesses didn't have or even think they needed an online presence, and the most visited website at the time was AOL.

Acquiring new clients in the early days required some out-of-the-box thinking. Denver was in a booming development stage at the time, with lofts, condos, and apartments being built all over town. I would drive around taking down the phone numbers of any development that didn't have a website on their signage. Then I'd pretend to be someone from New York or San Francisco moving to Denver who had heard of their project and, of course, ask for the domain of their website to learn more about the development and available units. When they responded with a lack of a website and offered to mail brochures, I would politely decline and occasionally question how serious the developer was if they didn't have a site. After a series of these calls over a few weeks, I would show up at the sales office to pitch a website. This was just one of the different techniques I applied in the early years.

Through two decades of highs and lows, Zenman grew into a globally recognized leader in the digital space. Our clients included an airline, several Fortune 500 companies, rock stars, and a unicorn (Ibotta, a startup that achieved a billion-dollar valuation) that we helped from inception to a two-billion-dollar publicly traded company. During my years running the agency, Zenman had some incredible runs of success, along with our share of dark times that nearly killed me. After 23 years in the game, I made a choice to get off the treadmill and start living my *Ikigai* (reason for being).

The process wasn't easy, but life has little ways of nudging you in the right direction if you don't fight the universe. I had a moment of clarity in 2017 when the realization hit me that the business that had been built through blood, sweat, and tears throughout my entire adult life was a machine that traded my time for money. I was selling the only finite resource in my possession...my time.

That day, there was a shift. I stopped designing and marketing products for other people. My passion and skills went into designing tools that helped people reach their full potential. The first product was the OAK Journal, a 90-day structured journal designed around my daily, weekly, and quarterly routines. As I started building and selling direct-to-consumer products, two things happened. First, the OAK Journal made it into the hands of several leaders all over Asia, and I was invited to do a speaking tour in Malaysia, Thailand, Indonesia, Singapore, and Vietnam. But they didn't want to hear me talk about the latest online trends; the request was for the methodology shared in the tool I had created.

The second was even more serendipitous. At a leadership conference in Peru I met a man from Argentina named Dani. One day he called me out of the blue to say that he wanted to buy an agency in the United States. My response was to start to tell him about the different agencies I knew in town, but he cut me off to say, "No, I want to buy your agency."

A few months later, Zenman was acquired by an exceptional organization. The merger took care of our clients and gave me an off-ramp that allowed me to transition into the next chapter. A year later, my earnout was finished, and after a sacred mushroom journey in Joshua Tree to cut any ties my ego had to the agency, I closed that door, enabling me to walk through the next one.

Now I spend my time writing books or keynote speaking. On the way to a recent event in Lake Tahoe, I was driving from

Colorado to Nevada. My oldest son had just graduated from eighth grade, and his Continuation Ceremony was held in the evening, the night before I was scheduled to speak. The timing meant that there were no available flights, so I drove through the night to make it to my talk. Just before sunrise, I fell asleep and my 4Runner crossed the middle line and scraped a truck and trailer coming the opposite direction head-on at 70 mph. Both tires and rims on the driver's side exploded on impact as they stuck out a couple of inches from the body of the truck, and it tore the door handles off. It was a miracle the crash wasn't a head-on collision that would have likely been fatal. The accident left me in shock for two days, but miraculously I walked away without a scratch. It took a series of cabs, flights, and hitched rides, but somehow I managed to make it to the event to do my first keynote in a clinical state of shock.

On the flight home, the second miracle occurred. I received a message from an acquisitions editor at John Wiley & Sons that this book was a green light. Maybe there was a reason the accident wasn't an inch to the left, which is why I am still here. Perhaps it was to share some of the concepts that have helped me through my entrepreneurial journey to help you, dear reader, find and live your Ikigai.

1

Begin

"Each morning, we are born again.
What we do today is what matters most."

—Buddha

1

Shoshin

Shoshin (初心) is a Zen Buddhist concept conveying a **beginner's mind**. It refers to having a perspective of openness, enthusiasm, and lack of preconceptions, even at an advanced level, just as a beginner would. To the beginner, there are many possibilities, whereas to the expert, there are few or possibly only one. Having a beginner's mind when reading this book and in your day-to-day life will result in exponential growth personally and professionally.

When someone is a genuine novice, their mind is unobstructed and available, like a kid discovering something for the first time. Over our lives, we develop knowledge and expertise, which can make our minds inherently more closed. Don't fall into the trap of thinking, "I already know how to do this."

A risk comes with believing we are an expert in anything. We overlook or ignore the facts contradicting what we learned previously and yield to the information confirming our current approach. We think we're learning, but we are cherry-picking through information and conversations, waiting to hear something corresponding to our existing ideology or prior understanding, and cherry-picking information to justify our current behaviors and beliefs. Most people want something other than new information; they want validating facts that reinforce existing beliefs.

In his book *Zen Mind, Beginner's Mind*, Zen master Shunryu Suzuki said, "In the beginner's mind, there are many possibilities, but in the expert's, there are few." When we believe we are experts in anything, we must pay more attention, not less. If you are familiar with 95 percent of the details on any topic, you must listen carefully to pick up on the remaining 5 percent.

There are a few valuable ways to find your beginner's mind and embrace the concept of shoshin.

Let Go of the Desire to Win Arguments

If someone makes a statement you believe is false during a discussion, embrace releasing the urge to correct it. Letting go of your need to show others how smart you are opens the possibility of learning something new. We will touch more on this in the chapter on Right Speech (Chapter 10).

Try the perspective of curiosity with topics in which you have extensive experience. Examine everything using an entirely different approach with an open mind. ***Minds are like parachutes; they don't work if they are closed.***

Listen More than You Speak

We think faster than we can speak. On average, a person speaks between 135 and 175 words per minute, but we can process up to 500 words per minute. Most people impatiently wait to speak while thinking of what to say next, rather than engaging in active listening. This is exasperating in business because, as leaders, we are looked up to as problem solvers, which leads to members of the team not speaking up and sharing their ideas.

You want to be surrounded by a variety of differing opinions to reach the best possible outcome. Abraham Lincoln appointed allies as well as past political rivals that he bested to win the Republican nomination for president to his cabinet to intentionally welcome opposing views into making some of the most important decisions in American history. These included William H. Seward as secretary of state, Salmon P. Chase as secretary of the treasury, and General Edward Bates as attorney general. His cabinet also included Edwin Stanton, who was a lifelong member of the Democratic party, showing that he was willing to work with anyone who was in favor of maintaining the Union.

Release the Need to Problem-Solve for Others

High achievers can feel an overwhelming desire to deliver value to those around them. Even though the intention is positive, constantly speaking rather than actively listening can limit our personal growth.

Very few people want to be told what to do when they are facing a challenge or opportunity. When we give advice, it can do more harm than good. If you constantly feel the need to add value by sharing advice, it can lead to adverse or even catastrophic results. What worked for your challenges might be different from the solution for others. Sharing our experiences rather than telling others how to solve their problems empowers us without limiting options.

As Socrates said, "The only true wisdom is in knowing that you know nothing."

2

The Four Noble Truths

"Pain pushes us to find out what really drives the world around us, and if it leads us to discover the laws of the hidden potential and imprints, it is the best thing that ever could have happened to us."
—The Diamond Cutter *by Geshe Michael Roach*

The Four Noble Truths are the foundation of Buddhism, which provides insights into the cause of our suffering and the path to liberation. Not understanding these truths means we sleepwalk through this life destined to repeat the same mistakes, not realizing that they are the cause of our suffering. These same Noble Truths also translate well to business situations.

A Quick Introduction to the Four Noble Truths

The Four Noble Truths, in summary, are as follows:

- Dukkha, the problem
- Samudāya, the cause
- Nirodha, the realization that there is a remedy
- Magga, the path to the cessation of suffering

Dukkha: The Truth of Suffering

The first Noble Truth, Dukkha, means "unease" and is commonly translated as "suffering," "unhappiness," or "pain." (How's that for a fun start to Buddhism: Life is suffering. Trust me, it gets a lot better, but it requires getting on the right path—and we'll get to that.) Dukkha comes in all shapes and sizes, but the three prominent kinds of suffering align with the first three sights Siddhartha Gautama (who would become the Buddha) saw the first time he left his palace.

Siddhartha was born the son of a king and lived a luxurious, sheltered life until, at 29 years old, he left the confines of his palace. The suffering he witnessed as he ventured outside his residence for the first time were a man bent with old age, another afflicted with sickness, and finally, death in the form of a corpse being carried to cremation. Siddhartha also witnessed a monk in deep meditation under a tree, which would be his chosen path—a road less traveled.

(Interesting fact: The three forms of suffering—old age, sickness, and death—and the monk in meditation, which Siddhartha Gautama witnessed, are known as the Four Signs. These signs are significant in Buddhism because they represent the realities of life that led Siddhartha to seek a path to the cessation of suffering.)

Buddha found that suffering went beyond the three examples he witnessed that day. Life is simply hard at times; not only does it fail to meet our expectations most of the time, but it is also sometimes downright woeful. Even when we achieve our goals and gain the object of our desire, whether it's in a new car, clothes, or other material possessions, the reward is short-lived. For some reason, most of us are never happy. We keep moving the goalpost and telling ourselves, "I'll be happy when I scale my business" or "when I can afford to buy a bigger house," but we are chasing happiness in places where it can't be found. The profound reality of life is that most of us won't get what we want, and even if we do, we can end up losing it one day.

The universe will always say "yes" to you. If you tell the universe, "I want to have money," it will deliver, but generally in the manner of a monkey's paw wish. The universe will deliver your "want" while you continue to suffer from desire when the head and heart are not aligned. That is the first Noble Truth, Dukkha.

Life is unsatisfactory, and suffering is an inescapable fact of existence. It encapsulates all aspects of life, from our physical body to our emotional and mental health. All sentient beings will experience a variety of suffering from the time of our birth and throughout our lives. When it comes to business, Dukkha can be a wide variety of things, ranging from something as traumatic as facing shutting down a business to something as insignificant as losing your keys when you're late for a meeting. The size of the suffering is not relevant; Dukkha can be many levels of dissatisfaction, discomfort, or stress.

> *Birth is suffering, aging is suffering, illness is suffering, death is suffering; union with what is displeasing is suffering; separation from what is pleasing is suffering; not to get what one wants is suffering; in brief, the five aggregates subject to clinging are suffering.*
>
> —*Buddha*

Dukkha is actually an essential aspect of life. How could we feel joy if we didn't know the opposite? There can be no left if there is no right. We need to experience both as part of the human experience to grow.

Samudāya: The Truth of the Cause of Suffering

Suffering, in its essence, is caused by desire, *tanhā*. Desire pertains to craving material possessions, pleasure, vanity, and everlastingness—the desire for reality to be different. It is not craving the wrong things that creates suffering, but rather the desire itself that creates Dukkha. Buddha taught that the root of suffering comes in three forms, which he described as the Three Poisons:

1. Greed and desire
2. Ignorance
3. Hatred

This does not mean we shouldn't set goals for ourselves, but rather think of them as direction instead of using them to keep score in life. It's essential not to compare ourselves to others because that is one recipe for perpetual suffering. The material and sensory pleasures we crave create a vicious cycle that can never be satisfied, no matter how successful we are.

Nirodha: The Truth of the Cessation of Suffering

Cessation of suffering occurs by breaking the cycle of craving and desire. By releasing our thirst for more, we can end our suffering. Once we shift from an "I want" to an "I am" mindset, our hearts and minds align, allowing us to accomplish anything. When our mind is set on a desire (probably influenced by society) that isn't in alignment with our heart, we will struggle to accomplish to reach the goal.

Magga: The Truth of the Path That Leads to the End of Suffering

The Noble Eightfold Path can lead to the end of suffering. This is also known as the Middle Way, which helps us avoid the extremes of self-denial and self-indulgence.

> *There is a middle way between the extremes of indulgence and self-denial, free from sorrow and suffering. This is the way to peace and liberation in this very life.*
>
> *—Buddha*

This book will explore each aspect of the Noble Eightfold Path, both in its influence on our personal lives and in how it applies to business. All eight aspects are followed with a chapter (or two) on a Buddhist concept that can be applied to modern business. In this chapter, I briefly discuss the Four Noble Truths as they pertain to business.

Dukkha in Business

As an entrepreneur, I experienced tremendous feast or famine over the 23 years of running my business. Agency life can be brutally stressful, and my particular business was service-based, which created challenges in the form of accurate forecasting. We built websites for some of the largest brands in the world, like RE/MAX, Frontier Airlines, and the Lumineers, but because the majority of our work was project-based rather than on retainer, we needed MRR (monthly recurring revenue). Dukkha (suffering) for me was either cash flow, clients, or people.

Cash Flow

Having to tell your employees the company is not going to make payroll is suffering at the highest level—something I hope never happens to you. We experienced issues with cash flow at my agency for two reasons:

- The first reason was a good problem to have: The company was growing, and we needed money to scale quickly. When expanding any organization, try to do it in a sustainable way. It is plausible that a business scales itself into closing its doors forever; this continues to happen again and again. A plethora of factors can decimate an organization, such as rapid overexpansion, building a product you are sure will sell only to find out you missed the mark and there is no demand, or maybe something completely out of your control, like a global pandemic.

- The second reason we encountered a cash flow crisis was due to a lack of sales. The lion's share of the agency's overhead was the extremely talented people whom we highly compensated. Delivering consistently exceptional work required a diverse team of creatives, developers, and operations, which made the agency's monthly overhead steep. Talent was getting paid whether or not they had billable work to do, and during the Great Recession (2009 in particular), I lost six figures a month trying to keep the doors open. In retrospect, I could have cut the headcount, but I felt the team was worth fighting for, which caused me to personally lose an exorbitant of money, putting both my agency and my home at risk.

It wasn't always doom and gloom. In fact, the good times outlasted the bad over the two decades, but there is a strange phenomenon in business (and in poker): Winning feels half as good, and losing feels twice as bad.

To remove Dukkha (suffering) from your business, the first and most important step is understanding the financials.

This doesn't mean a 30,000-foot view or a gut instinct. What are the details regarding COGs (cost of goods sold)? How many months of overhead do you have in cash reserves? Do you have a model that allows you to adjust sales or add team members to see how it impacts profits? Are there accurate forecasting models in place? When an organization has clarity into the finances, it empowers them to deploy resources into growth, research, and development or to take some chips off the table entirely while the business is profitable.

Clients

Customers can be challenging in any of the many categories of businesses. From my personal experience, they are the most difficult in the agency services world. Client suffering can take many forms, from over-demanding ones who can't wait five minutes after sending an email to completely unresponsive ones who create bottlenecks that impact multiple other projects. Unfortunately, no business can survive sans customers. It is, however, possible to attract and nurture ideal clients.

Attracting the Right Client.   The most straightforward way to remove suffering is to attract the right customer to the business. Everything from a business atmosphere, culture, and pricing of products or services to the places a company advertises can help you find your ideal client.

Sometimes you must work up to the level you want to play at. My first customers at the agency were not airlines and rock stars. In fact, it was the opposite. The first paying site I built was for an asbestos and poisonous mold abatement company. We treated that company like royalty and created a website the client loved, which accurately presented them as the heroes they are.

Treating every client as an opportunity to deliver your best work has two benefits:

- First, it builds a reputation for keeping commitments to your customers by providing the goods or services on or before the deadline. To this day, it baffles me how many organizations create suffering because they lack the discipline to deliver on time. Under-promise and overdeliver. Actions speak louder than words, and a business's reputation is more visible today than ever before. Potential customers can read about the quality of your products and the experience of dealing with your staff. Potential employees can see how previous team members rate the organization as a workplace when deciding if they should apply to your company or the competition.

- Second, always doing the best possible work for every single customer creates case studies of successful projects that will help close new clients. It doesn't matter if you are building a portfolio of work to showcase or selling a widget. The quality of the product or service delivered is paramount to growth and reputation. When you have an established credibility for consistently delivering excellence, it will attract the right customers to your business.

Occasionally, the wrong client walks into our business, and we sell them our product or service. Know that it is entirely acceptable and at times essential to fire a client. This can be as simple as knowing when to cut off someone who has had too many cocktails at your restaurant or as complex as involving lawyers to untangle intricate legal contracts.

We signed a client at the agency during a prolonged slow stretch. That meant I had staff on the beach (an agency term for not doing billable work), and cash was extremely tight.

The client embraced our core values, the project processes during the sales and contracting phase, and understood our pricing. Zenman had a reputation for three things:

1. Being extremely process-driven (which was an oddity for most creative shops)

2. Consistently delivering exceptional creative work with quantifiable results (Yes, we won a ton of awards for the various brands, websites, and so on that the agency created, but our clients knew we would perpetually deliver on their business objectives.)

3. Being expensive (You get what you pay for.)

When it came to the first meeting, the client threw a tremendous curveball by introducing a "majority partner" who proceeded to steamroll over our agenda. He questioned our pricing, process, and timeline for delivering the project. As a highly process-driven company, we had signed contracts and one-third of the project cost in the bank before we would schedule our project kickoff meeting. The Zenman team spends a week researching the client and their competition to be thoroughly informed and prepared before the first meeting. What should have been a two-hour discovery session devolved into a full-day eight-hour meltdown that included bullish attempts to renegotiate the cost and timeline. After wasting a whole day butting heads with someone who clearly was not a fit to work with Zenman, we fired them as clients. I remember the exact moment it happened. The majority partner's bullying tactics hadn't worked, so in frustration he yelled at my CEO, "Listen, little missy, let me tell you how it's going to go!"

That was it. My CEO, a badass businesswoman, calmly got up from the meeting and proceeded to get the company checkbook from her office, then replied, "No, let me tell *you* how it's going to go." We fired them and reimbursed the entire deposit.

Suddenly, their posture changed to apologies, asking if we would continue the project. The answer was a resounding "No." Writing the check and refunding their deposit was brutal; we really needed the funds, but it was crystal clear that the client would have been a nightmare, and more importantly, they would have abused my team, which I couldn't abide.

Our target personas had one consistent trait—someone who values our expertise and is willing to pay for it. Understand who your ideal customer is and build the brand that attracts them.

Getting the Right Clarity.   In business and life, clarity is vital to reaching our full potential. This includes everything from understanding the company's 10-year BHAG (Big Hairy Audacious Goal) to knowing its return policy. As an organization scales in size, this becomes even more necessary.

Imagine your organization as a rowboat. In the beginning, you have three people in the boat, all rowing in the same direction. Progress is slowly going toward your goal, but you need to be quicker, so you add more to the team. Eventually, dozens of people are frantically rowing but have yet to make significant progress. This happens when everyone in the boat is rowing in a different direction.

Take time to align your business with long-term and short-term goals that are crystal clear. Create and declare the company's 3-, 5-, and 10-year goals. The simple act of writing them down doubles the probability of accomplishing them. Start with the 10-year goal and be as detailed as possible. Answer questions like:

- What is your revenue?
- What is your EBITDA (earnings before interest, taxes, depreciation, and amortization)?

- Do you own the real estate your business occupies?
- How many employees work at the company?
- What states or countries have you expanded operations to?
- What awards or patents has the company received?

Most people overestimate what can be done in a year but underestimate what can be done in a decade. Once you have a clear vision of where you will be in 10 years, you can create a roadmap to reaching that goal. Answer the same questions five years from now. Where do you need to be in order to be on track? Repeat this process for three years in the future. Once we have clarity around our long-term vision, it's time to set the short-term objectives.

Immediate objectives that take over a week to complete should be broken into SMART goals (simple, measurable, attainable, relevant, and timebound) with no more than a 90-day timeline. Several studies have shown that anything longer than three months for projects is less likely to be successful. This happens for various reasons, such as other projects that take priority, personnel change mid-project, and even simple procrastination because the deadline is too far in the future. If a project is too extensive to complete in 90 days, break it into multiple deliverables that can be completed in three months. Anything that takes less than a week would become a "to-do" and assigned to a single owner.

Frequently communicate the organization's long-term vision and current short-term projects, including progress (good or bad) on both. Create KPIs (key performance indicators) that are leading indicators of success to track weekly or monthly and include these metrics in weekly meetings with the leadership team and quarterly town halls for the entire company. By clearly and frequently communicating, you get everyone rowing the boat in the same direction.

People on Your Team

Anything is possible with the right people working together toward a common goal if everyone is acting in their zone of genius. However, even the most talented teams can only succeed when people are in the right roles within an organization. For example, the most gifted software developer is probably a horrible salesperson. They are exceptional developers because they spend 10,000 hours writing code in a dark room, not attending networking or social events that a solid salesperson would have spent their time on. Know your people's strengths and elevate them to do their best work.

It starts with hiring the right people for your team. This can be one of the most challenging parts of any organization's growth, but with discipline and a few simple techniques, it will help increase the chances of hiring correctly. Look at any potential hire in these three categories:

1. Are they a fit for the role (does their personality align with the job)?
2. Can they do the job (do they have the skillset required for the role)?
3. Do they align with our vision and core values (are they our people)?

Are They a Fit for the Role?   Let's start with whether a potential hire fits the role they applied for. It is finding where an individual's true strengths and weaknesses have never been more accessible. By utilizing personality tests like Myers-Briggs, DISC, 16 Personalities, and Enneagram, it's possible to identify people who are wired best to accomplish specific roles within any organization. Each modality has a personality type best suited for the different job categories, so you can see if someone is built for the role or simply playing the part. It's easy to fool someone in a job interview, but it's much harder to fake a personality test.

Set your company and every employee up for success by finding each individual's unique superpower, then let them thrive by using it. This approach also allows you to build effective teams by pairing the different personality types to elevate the entire group's collective performance and decision-making.

Can They Do the Job? Once you have the right personality fit for the role, the next step is determining if they have the skills to fulfill the position's duties. This was another area where agency hiring felt like the most challenging type of business to hire for. When a candidate applies for a creative director position and shows off the portfolio of work they taught as their creation, it's hard to really know how much of the work was indeed theirs. For example, I have personally met seven different individuals who claim to have come up with "The Most Interesting Man in the World" Dos Equis advertising campaign.

How can you genuinely determine a candidate's skillset? First, always do your due diligence when checking references. This doesn't mean just calling the shortlist of references on the applicant's resume. Do your homework and talk to the people from their previous job not listed as references to get an authentic perspective on their past work performance. A good rule of thumb is that if they list the person as a reference, it will be a positive referral, so dig a few layers deeper to get a truly accurate representation.

Create tests to see how the candidate performs tasks essential to the role. This can be done for sales jobs that include mock calls as part of the interview process or even for software developers. One of the premier software consulting companies, Pivotal Labs, started their interview process with an RPI (Rob's Pair Interview). Pivotal was an Agile software development shop that utilized pair programming. Every project had one or more pairs of developers who sat together all day writing software collaboratively. One screen, two keyboards, and exceptional code produced by two highly skilled developers. Pivotal was famous for creating unrivaled quality software using the Agile development method. The only way to guarantee world-class code was by employing the absolute best developers to write it. You did the RPI while paired with the company's founder, Rob. He assessed how the developer approached a fixed set of challenges, scoring them on the code written. If the candidate fell below an A+ score at any time, the interview was over, and Rob would share constructive feedback to help the applicant grow, but they wouldn't make the cut to be hired.

Do They Align with the Vision and Core Values?

Finally, if the applicant is wired for the role and has the skillset to accomplish the job tasks, the final critical element is whether they align with the company's vision and values. I have seen top performers correctly removed from organizations because they failed to act in alignment with the vision and values. Core values are a filter that allows us to look at our decisions within a business and in our personal lives. How do we indeed find out if a candidate embodies the values? There are tests for personality types to see if someone is wired to do a particular role. Each job can have a test to measure the applicant's skillset, and yes, it's possible to create a test for core values.

My favorite example of a core value test is a company whose number one value was "Take Ownership." The test was a hallway—to be more specific, a straight hallway about 10 meters long with no windows. At the far end of the hallway was a door to a conference room that also had no windows. Halfway down the hallway, a piece of paper was balled up on the floor less than a meter away from a trash can. Since the hallway had no windows, the interviewee wholeheartedly believes no one is watching them walk "to" the interview. What they don't realize is that the hallway, or, to be more specific, the balled-up piece of paper, is the only non-negotiable part of the interview. If they pick up the paper and place it in the trashcan, that person passes the core value test and is hired over 95 percent of the time.

With the right people on the team, it's possible to change the world.

Samudāya in Business

The second Noble Truth, Samudāya, is caused by cravings or tanha (which translates to "thirst"). It is our desire and ignorance that lead to our suffering while we continuously yearn for more than we are currently experiencing. That translates into comparing our business success to the results of others, which is a recipe for disaster.

In Buddhism, tanha (thirst) refers to craving physical pleasure, material possessions, and immortality. In business, tanha is continuously shifting the goalposts of success. Many successful entrepreneurs suffer even during unfathomable success because they have created the myth "I'll be happy when I hit $10,000,000 in revenue," or "I'll be happy when I have my exit." When they finally do reach their goal, happiness is not waiting like a pot of gold at the end of the rainbow. Most founders have an existential crisis after even the most profitable acquisitions due to a loss of identity.

The right mindset is "I am," not "I will be." Right now is the only moment that matters, so be present. This shift to "I am" also helps generate the energy that attracts synchronicity toward the right path.

Samudāya and ego caused me to overspend in fat times, leading to cash flow issues quickly when work dried up. My agency had all the bells and whistles that I justified at the time, saying, "We need to impress our clients." Zenman had everything from pricey original art on the walls to custom furniture built for the overpriced hip co-working space that was lined with vintage collectible Star Wars Lego sets. I even had an original FunHouse pinball machine inside my office, not inside the agency; it was my personal pinball machine. Agencies typically have creative workplaces, but when I look back at the waste I justified as culture, it causes me Dukkha.

Nirodha in Business

The third Noble Truth is Nirodha, and that is curable. When we stop comparing ourselves to others, it's easy to detach ourselves from the material desires perpetuating suffering. It is acceptable to be wildly successful in business if your intentions are pure. Success enables you to change the world for the better, but it also drives some to commit atrocities against animals, humanity, and even Mother Earth.

Contrast this with Jimmy Donaldson, or as your kids know him on YouTube, MrBeast. Jimmy has used his reach and financial resources to accomplish life-changing philanthropic initiatives. He has built 100 wells in Africa, cured blindness for 1,000 people, rescued dogs, helped 2,000 amputees walk again, saved an orphanage, and donated $30 million in free food. Yes, he also had a chocolate bar brand, MrBeast merch, and does a lot of content unrelated to philanthropy for his channel, but most importantly, he uses his success to make the world a better place.

Compare that with the makers of pharmaceutical drugs that are known to be harmful or addictive and are pushed for profit, or consider the industries that knowingly destroy the environment. Choose to be a force for good with your success.

Magga in Business

The fourth Noble Truth is Magga, which is the path that leads us away from suffering. As mentioned earlier this is known as the Noble Eightfold Path or the Middle Way.

The Noble Eightfold Path is:

- Right Understanding
- Right Thought
- Right Speech
- Right Action
- Right Livelihood
- Right Effort
- Right Mindfulness
- Right Concentration

We will explore each of the Eightfold Path's elements, followed by a Zen technique to help serve as your compass along the journey. The elements of the Eightfold Path are meant to be done in parallel rather than in order. The eight elements are broken down into three sections: Wisdom (Understanding, Thought), Morality (Speech, Action, Livelihood), and Mind (Effort, Mindfulness, Concentration).

Tool: Visualizing the Future

Creating a clear visualization of the future aligns your vibrations with that potential. Exercises like vision boards are powerful tools to establish a clear foresight of the imagined outcome. Combining images and words is an effective tool to align your energy

(continued)

(*continued*)

with your intention. When you are imagining your future, think about 10 years from today. Close your eyes and think about three categories of your life: business, personal, and family/relationships. Answer the following questions with the "I am" mindset as if you are currently experiencing this future. Provide as much detail as possible, and while writing the answers, see yourself in the scene you are describing.

Date (10 years from today): _____

What is the gross company revenue? _____
Profit?_____

What are you most proud of in your professional life?
_____
_____
_____
_____

Describe your average workday from start to finish.
_____
_____
_____
_____

List any recognitions or awards the company has received.
_____
_____
_____
_____

Who do you spend the most time with?

_____
_____
_____
_____

How do your family and closest friends describe you to others?

_____
_____
_____
_____

What are you the most proud of in your personal life?

_____
_____
_____
_____

Where do you live (country, state, city, etc.), and *why* do you live there?

_____
_____
_____
_____

Describe your house in detail (inside and outside).

_____
_____
_____
_____

(continued)

(*continued*)

Describe your perfect day from the moment you wake up
until the moment you fall asleep.

_____

_____

_____

_____

_____

_____

_____

_____

_____

_____

_____

_____

_____

_____

_____

_____

_____

_____

_____

_____

_____

_____

_____

_____

_____

_____

_____

_____

3

Finding Your Way

When we take responsibility for our current circumstances, we shift from blaming others to taking control of our lives. It is easy to diminish the fact that we are responsible for where we currently reside on our path today, but it's still the truth. The one person in control of your life is you.

The magic of living your best possible life is simple: Embrace 100 percent accountability for the whole shebang. Yes, I do mean your entire life is in your control. For our whole lives the thoughts we have are planting seeds that will grow into reality at an unforeseen future date. Even the subtlest negative idea in our mind creates an impression that will eventually come to fruition. Whether good or bad, abundant or scarce, our vibrations attract like frequencies that attract and bring them into our lives.

If you are struggling with financial stress today, ask yourself, "What choices have I made that created my current situation?" Someone who struggles with money stress might have challenges living within their means and spending within their budget, or they might have rejected opportunities to increase their ability to earn what they deserve through the Right Livelihood (see Chapter 15).

Perhaps it is our relationships or lack of them that is causing pain. How have our actions led to the place where we are hurting from a toxic relationship or complete lack of companionship?

The most straightforward example is our health. If you are obese, it is due to dietary choices made over many years, along with a lack of proper activity to keep your body healthy. The same can be said about ingesting excessive amounts of alcohol or polluting your lungs with smoke and addictive chemicals. A wise man once said, "If knowledge equaled results, everyone would have six-pack abs." We all know what it takes to be mentally and physically fit, but most people never take action.

Take comfort in knowing that today, you are precisely where you need to be to find your path. Everyone's route is different, but the one constant thing is how winding each of our lives will be while we search. When we take responsibility for our current station in life, it empowers us to find direction.

Finding Our Way: The Unalome

The Unalome is a Buddhist and Hindu symbol that represents our path to enlightenment (see Figure 3.1). This metaphor for how chaotic and directionless life can feel shows both the challenging times in life and the peace that can be achieved through finding our noble path. Each of the three sections in this sacred symbol represents a stage in our life. At birth, we are inexperienced and search for direction. Throughout our journey, we continue to make errors that become learning opportunities for finding our individual path until we finally awaken. With that clarity, we have direction and will eventually reach enlightenment.

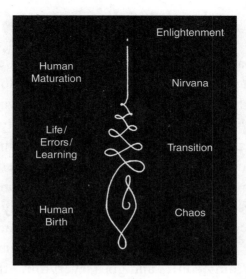

FIGURE 3.1 The Unalome represents how winding our path will be from beginning to end.

Source: Keith Roberts.

Life is a twisty road for a reason. The **pursuit of happiness** is considered an unalienable right in the United States Declaration of Independence (the other two are "life" and "liberty"). Note that it doesn't state that "happiness" is a right bestowed on all sentient beings. It states that we have the undeniable right to **pursue** happiness. Along the way, we will all encounter challenges, failure, heartbreak, joy, love, and success. We have to love the journey, not just the result. As Kobe Bryant said, "Those times when you get up early and you work hard. Those times when you stay up late, and you work hard. Those times when you don't feel like working, you're too tired, and you don't want to push yourself, but you do it anyway. That is actually the dream. That's the dream. It's not the destination; it's the journey. And if you guys can understand that, then what you'll see happen is that you won't accomplish your dreams. Your dreams won't come true. Something greater will."

Addressing Self-Sabotage

Finding our path is hard enough, but staying on course is even more audacious throughout our lifetime. After doing deep personal work to find our Ikigai (see Chapter 16), we still have the risk that we will lose our way. The one certainty is that all of us will face challenges at different stages throughout our entire lives. It could come in the form of business challenges, financial stress, our health, and that of those we love, along with death. Impermanence is the concept that life constantly changes, and it states that everything that comes to be will eventually pass away. Buddha taught that nothing in the universe is essential and that everything comes and goes, everything that lives must die, and everything created will crumble.

Those of us who have experienced trauma in our youth have another conundrum. Someone who experiences stress growing up will develop coping mechanisms out of necessity. It could be from a shockingly long list of events that shape our personality early in life. The wounded child of an abusive addict parent might develop a default response to lie or embellish out of fear of being harmed. As that person grows up, they don't evolve naturally out of the wounded child response. As an example, an adult child of a person with an addiction who is asked at work if a project is done could respond dishonestly that it is complete, even if it's far from it. Latent habits that are done subconsciously have the potential to sabotage any situation. These patterns are complex to break and require a shift from the wounded child to a functional adult mindset.

Some people may develop self-sabotaging behaviors even without experiencing trauma in their youth. You can engage in actions (or lack of action) that create problems and slow down progress, and the ultimate outcome is not reaching your full potential. Examples of self-sabotaging behaviors include:

- Missing deadlines
- Self-medication
- Procrastination
- Arrogance
- Neglecting health (diet, activity, etc.)
- Binge shopping
- Negative self-talk
- Perfectionism
- Financial neglect

The preeminent mystery most of us face is that we are unaware of the behavior until it is already causing damage to our lives. The magic is in how we identify our harmful actions at the onset to avoid turning a good situation into a bad one.

What is your canary in the coal mine? That saying comes from the Gold Rush era and refers to the practice of miners taking small birds with them to gauge the carbon monoxide levels in the mines as an early warning sign. The birds have a rapid breathing rate, much smaller lungs, and higher metabolism than humans, so when a bird lost consciousness and fell off its perch, the miners knew the levels of oxygen had become unsafe, giving them time to take action and return to the surface before succumbing to the toxic air.

When we have self-awareness to be present every day, the signs of self-sabotage become apparent, and we just have to look. Make a list of the thoughts and actions that you associate with self-sabotaging behaviors. One example could be procrastination and how it impacts your business. Imagine that Q1 is booked solid with profitable business and the pipeline of prospects is robust. It is so strong, in fact, that the time to turn around proposals and respond promptly to inquiries becomes lackadaisical. Procrastination kicks in, and projects that had a high probability of closing are now lost due to a lack of confidence created by overpromising and under-delivering. **It is 1,000 times more applaudable to set realistic expectations and exceed them than to be even one minute late or fall 1 percent short of your commitments.**

This can be exasperating for those of us who experienced challenges in home life growing up. A common characteristic shared is being the "pleaser." Not only do pleasers often neglect their own needs for the needs of others, but another typical default response is to overpromise to try to make the other person happy. During my agency days at Zenman, I would over-commit in client meetings that would mortify my team. I would even promise deliverables ahead of the client's timeline with the goal of impressing them, but it would only backfire by burning out my team while not delivering our best work. Exceptional work takes time to create. We don't do our best work under pressure; it's a misconception. It's possible to crunch at deadline time, but you are not delivering the best possible work. We do the best work when we take our time, iterate, learn, and refine.

When it comes to deadlines imposed by clients, always understand the business case for the deliverable's due date. Is it based on an actual event like a product launch, or did the CMO just pull a random date to be aggressive with the project timeline?

Discovering the Middle Way

Once we identify and accept that we have fallen into negative behavior, the next step is to resolve the internal struggle that is creating the subconscious acts. Binge spending is a symptom, not an affliction. Ultimately, addressing the root cause is required to stop the patterns from recurring. Root causes include:

- Low self-esteem
- Fear of failure
- Imposter syndrome
- Trauma

These barriers that we face in our personal lives eventually bleed into the professional world. All humans are like a three-legged stool. One leg represents our personal life (physical and mental health), the second leg represents our relationships, and the third leg is our professional life. Just like a stool, if one or more legs of our life become unbalanced, eventually the entire stool (or our life) will come crashing down.

Start by understanding the need or void that self-sabotage is trying to fill. Sometimes it might feel like you have identified the root cause, but continue to peel back the layers until it truly hits home, and in that aha moment there is clarity around the source. Keep asking yourself "why" in the process. If you go through the tool at the end of this chapter to identify the core limiting belief and the answer is "I'm not worthy," ask yourself when you first had that feeling. Explore the earliest memories of experiencing those emotions. Did a parent or teacher ever say, "You're not smart enough" or "You're not talented enough" to accomplish a particular thing? These early impressions are the seeds of our self-sabotage.

Jimmy Kwik suffered a severe brain injury at the age of five. One of his teachers referred to him in class in front of all the other students as "the boy with the broken brain." Imagine the negative impact that being ridiculed by your teacher in front of your peers has on a child. Luckily for Jimmy, he had a mentor who inspired him to learn about the human brain and how it's possible to rewire it. Jimmy Kwik is now considered one of the world's top brain coaches and is a best-selling author. Pinpointing the root cause—growing up thinking your brain was broken—helped lead him to becoming a master of the human mind, empowering millions to recall, read, think, and learn faster. His path required identifying the limiting belief that had been ingrained in his psyche at the earliest age so that he could turn it from a perceived weakness to a powerful strength.

I left no stone unturned in the search for my path. My quest took me from the jungles of Peru, retracing ancient Incan trails to Machu Picchu, to sacred sites all over Asia, Joshua Tree, Death Valley, and Black Rock City. One thing I can share with you is that the longer we have been on the wrong path, the harder it is to break out of old patterns. Our thoughts become actions, making it vitally important that we understand ourselves at a fundamental level and address our weaknesses by establishing healthy routines.

Here are some of the indispensable core techniques to finding our Middle Way:

- Identify and remove triggers
- Practice mindfulness
- Develop positive habits
- Have a support system
- Practice positive affirmations

Moderation is the key, and that is the Middle Way. The life of Siddhartha Gautama (Buddha) is a perfect example. Born into a life of royalty and luxury, Siddhartha renounced his title as prince when he saw the suffering of humanity with his own eyes.

He became a monk and attempted to reach enlightenment through extreme austerity, but after meditating for long periods while consuming only a single grain of rice each day, Buddha realized that the radical approach was not the path.

Also known as the Noble Eightfold Path (see Chapter 4), the Middle Way teaches that we should not indulge in excess but also that we don't need to practice extreme self-depreciation to reach enlightenment. Buddha spent the rest of his life teaching balance over extremism with the Four Noble Truths (see Chapter 2) and the Noble Eightfold Path.

Tool: Thoughts and Actions = Core Belief

Every day, each of us experiences negative thoughts and/or engages in actions that are self-destructive. To break the cycle of negative energy, we have first to identify them to get to our core limiting beliefs. Once we have identified these, the next step is to rewire your brain to positive thoughts, actions, and empowering beliefs.

What negative or limiting thoughts do you have (daily, weekly, or infrequently)? List all thoughts or feelings that are negative or that come from a scarcity perspective.

_____

_____

_____

_____

_____

_____

_____

_____

(continued)

(*continued*)

List the actions that are not constructive in living your best life. This can be anything from binge-watching to social media addiction, not keeping your commitments, or impulse online shopping.

_____

_____

_____

_____

_____

_____

_____

_____

_____

Review the thoughts and actions listed earlier and distill them into one limiting core belief that is at the center of everything you do that doesn't align with living your best life. (Examples: I am not worthy, I am not smart enough, I don't deserve love or friendship.)

_____

_____

Write the opposite upbeat version of your core belief. If you wrote, "I am not worthy," write "I am worthy." Turn the negative into the most positive iteration.

_____

_____

Take each negative thought listed earlier and change it to
the opposite positive statement. For example, if you wrote,
"I am not creative," restate it to "I am extremely creative."

_____

_____

_____

_____

_____

_____

_____

_____

_____

Do the same thing with your limiting actions. Restate
them into empowering actions.

_____

_____

_____

_____

_____

_____

_____

_____

Choose one or two from each list (positive thoughts and
actions) and consciously do them every day. Soon you will
break the powerful cycle, and the mind will shift uncon-
sciously to the right thoughts, actions, and core beliefs.

4

The Noble Eightfold Path

The fourth Noble Truth is Magga, the path that leads us away from suffering, which is also known as the Noble Eightfold Path. This was in the Buddha's first sermon after he attained enlightenment, to which he devoted the rest of his life. These practices are not steps to be done in order but in parallel in perpetuity.

It is said, "**There are only two mistakes along this way. You are not starting this one, and you are not bringing this one to the end.**" Each of these practices is as important to business as our personal lives, but as stated so eloquently, starting isn't enough; we must follow through to be successful.

Most people don't reach their full potential because success is disguised as hard work over prolonged periods of time. Overnight blockbusters are misconceived by most as what we should be trying to achieve. Still, we are fooled by the fraction of success stories (Gates, Zuckerberg, Jobs, Bezos) that are constantly in front of us, while what we *don't* see are the thousands upon thousands of shuttered businesses and bankruptcies. Overnight success is a myth. It takes grit to bring something from your mind to the marketplace.

The Noble Eightfold Path, which applies to all aspects of our lives including business, consists of these elements:

- Right Understanding (Samma ditthi)
- Right Thought (Samma sankappa)
- Right Speech (Samma vaca)
- Right Action (Samma kammanta)
- Right Livelihood (Samma ajiva)
- Right Effort (Samma vayama)
- Right Mindfulness (Samma sati)
- Right Concentration (Samma samadhi)

Let's dive deeper into each of the practices.

Right Understanding (*Samma Ditthi*)

The first step in the Eightfold Path is Right Understanding or Right View. This refers to how we view the world and everything in it. It creates the foundation for attaining the highest wisdom. We gain this wisdom by embracing impermanence while contemplating life, death, and Karma. How helpful would it be to the business if you made time to ponder the potential challenges an organization could face in the future? Now contemplate what's possible if you accept that everything that exists today will one day be no more.

Right Understanding means seeing the world and everything it is as it really is, not as we want it to be. This requires clearing our minds from misunderstanding and misguided thinking. With this perspective, we can liberate ourselves from the hardship caused by the wrong view. (Find out more in Chapter 5.)

Buddha said, "I must state clearly that my teaching is a method to experience reality and not reality itself, just as a finger pointing at the moon is not the moon itself. A thinking person makes use of the finger to see the moon. A person who only looks at the finger and mistakes it for the moon will never see the real moon."

Right Thought (*Samma Sankappa*)

Right Thought or Right Intent is the second practice on the Eightfold Path. This must come from your heart and involves recognizing the equality of all life and compassion for all that life, beginning with compassion for yourself. Thoughts of selfish desire, hate, and violence are due to a lack of wisdom. When we understand the laws of Karma and the cause of suffering, it's possible to live a life skillfully.

Right Thought commits one to a life of personal growth and ethical behavior, intentionally rejecting the vicious cycle of craving. By choosing the awakened perspective, we can look at any situation and see that it is neither good nor bad. It's impossible to know how lucky we can be in not getting what we want. There is an old story of unknown origin that illustrates this best.

Long ago, a humble farmer lived in a village on a small plot of land with his wife and only son. Their livelihood depended on the one horse they owned, the family's most essential and valuable possession. One morning, the farmer awoke to find that the horse had broken out of the stable and run away. Word spread through the small community, and his neighbors would stop to console the farmer. "It's horrible that you have lost your horse; how will you tend the fields?" Much to their bewilderment, the farmer replied simply, "Good, bad, who knows."

A few days later, the farmer arose to find that his horse had returned and brought with him a dozen wild stallions that now gathered in the stable. Word spread through the village, and again, all of his neighbors commented, this time praising his good fortune. "You are so lucky, those stallions are so valuable, you are the wealthiest man in the village now," to which the man again replied, "Good, bad, who knows." The very next day, the farmer's only son was attempting to break one of the stallions and was thrown, breaking his leg badly. Again, the farmer was consoled by everyone. "What a horrible tragedy; your son may never walk again." His stoic response continued to perplex: "Good, bad, who knows." His son's leg was set, and he was still bedridden weeks later when the army came through the village, drafting every able-bodied young man to fight on the front lines of a bloody conflict. The farmer's son, still unable to walk, was spared the inevitable death of war.

We always wonder if something that we perceive as unfavorable is actually the greatest possible gift we could receive. (Find out more in Chapter 8.)

Right Speech (*Samma Vaca*)

Abstain from harmful speech and cultivate healthy speech. Harmful speech includes lying, divisive speech, slander, and gossip. Practice speech that is true and beneficial and is spoken with good intentions. We should also not speak carelessly. Learn to speak at the right time and place, which almost always means listening more than talking.

When not adding something useful, practice Noble Silence. Noble silence is the concept of not speaking unnecessary words, which leads to more meaningful speech. Like my grandmother used to say (and yours probably did too), "If you can't say something nice, don't say anything at all."

Words spoken cannot be taken back. Being mindful of how we use our words in life and in business is one of the most significant choices we can make. Speech is powerful. Our words shape our minds and influence those around us. (Find out more in Chapter 10.)

Right Action (*Samma Kammanta*)

Right Action recognizes the need to take an ethical approach to life, intentionally regarding others and the world around us. It also includes doing no harm to ourselves in addition to not harming others. This includes neglecting our health (physical and mental), being irresponsible with our financial responsibilities, becoming addicted to substances, or engaging in unethical business practices.

Right Action encompasses the five tenets that were given by the Buddha: not to kill, not to steal, not to lie, not to engage in sexual misconduct, and not to take drugs or other intoxicants. This step on the path also includes fundamental care of the environment, with Right Action taken whenever possible to safeguard the world for future generations. This does not mean we can't enjoy life. Right Action includes truthfulness, moral business success, and healthy, loving sexual intimacy. (Find out more in Chapter 12.)

Right Livelihood (*Samma Ajiva*)

Right Livelihood (see Chapter 15) means abstaining from earning a living through a profession that brings harm to others or oneself. Buddha encouraged ethically positive business practices that share wisdom, create happiness, and alleviate suffering from others and themselves.

Buddha shared five professions through which we should *not* earn our livelihood:

1. Dealing in weapons
2. Human trade
3. Butchery
4. Intoxicants
5. Poisons

This is more complicated in the modern world, but all businesses become apparent when applying the five professions as a filter, and it's possible to determine if your profession is helping or harming society. Our goal in life should be to find one's Ikigai (see Chapter 16), which is a combination of two Japanese terms: *Iki* ("to live") and *Gai* ("reason"), so in other words, our "reason to live." When someone finds their Ikigai, they live a life of purpose and joy.

Right Effort (*Samma Vayama*)

Live in a state of wholesome thoughts, speech, and actions. Life is a continuous cycle of choices that are forks in the road for our Karma. Right Effort (or Diligence) aligns our intentions with compassion, cultivating them with balance and enthusiasm. It is not about striving for perfection but rather graceful refinement on our path. Buddha taught four aspects of Right Effort:

- Effort to prevent unwholesome qualities
- Effort to extinguish unwholesome qualities

- Effort to cultivate wholesome qualities
- Effort to strengthen wholesome qualities

In business, the Right Effort translates into how we spend our time and resources. Are we making progress toward the goal or wasting energy with distractions and engaging in the wrong activities? More importantly, the objective we are working toward aligns with our true purpose. Thich Nhat Hanh says, "Right Diligence is nourished by joy and interest. If your practice does not bring you joy, you are not practicing correctly." We should be doing work that brings us joy and purpose in our lives. (Find out more in Chapter 18.)

Right Mindfulness (*Samma Sati*)

Being present and focused on the current moment, not regretting the past or contemplating the future, is Right Mindfulness. It is being aware that our journey is the goal itself and being grateful for every day. Time is the only currency we spend without knowing how much we have left. Be mindful of your most valuable currency; since you can never check the remaining balance, spend your time as if each day were your last.

With clarity, we can identify destructive patterns in our lives and eliminate them. This means being actively mindful of the current moment in an accurate view unfiltered by expectations or desires. So much of human suffering comes from regretting the past, which we cannot change, or worrying about the future when the only thing that matters is the present moment. Find out more in Chapter 20.

Right Concentration (*Samma Samadhi*)

By clearing our mind's inner chatter and our ego, we can achieve the goals and life we are meant to achieve. This does *not* mean concentrating on the new Porsche you want to acquire; it means focusing on your life purpose with loving compassion. Right Concentration brings all factors of the Noble Eightfold Path into harmony, creating a state of awareness described as attentive, peaceful, and blissful.

Practicing Right Concentration builds a balanced state of mind that is less easily disturbed by the daily challenges we face. It brings harmony to the mind and aligns all aspects of the Eightfold Path. (Find out more in Chapter 22.)

Tool: Stop and Start List

Every one of us has behaviors that we need to stop and actions we need to start to be the best version of ourselves. Write a list of what you commit to beginning today and to stopping today. Maybe it's to eliminate a habit like smoking, drinking, or social media, or even to discontinue engaging with a toxic friend who is an energy vampire. Perhaps you need to start meditating, eating healthily, or working out.

Commit to *starting* today:

_____

_____

_____

_____

_____

_____

_____

_____

_____

_____

_____

Commit to *stopping* today:

_____

_____

_____

_____

_____

_____

_____

_____

_____

_____

Wisdom (*panna*)

"Zen is a path of liberation. It liberates you. It is freedom from the first step to the last. You are not required to follow any rules; you are required to find out your own rules and your own life in the light of awareness."

—Osho

CHAPTER

5

Right Understanding

Right Understanding or Right View is the overarching practice that informs all other aspects of the Noble Eightfold Path. Although the eight practices are not meant to be done in sequence, it's necessary to start with the Right Understanding, or our Actions, Speech, Thoughts, and so on will be misaligned. This serves as the compass of our individual path. Our view should not be obstructed by the desires that cause suffering (Samudāya—the Second Noble Truth; see Chapter 2) but formed through mindful observations.

There are three stages to Right Understanding. The first is learning by reading and studying texts. The second is understanding, which is repeated contemplation of what has been read. The third and most crucial stage is the liberation that comes with realizing the magic in the present moment through the practice of morality and mindfulness. Correct intentions are set when our thoughts are pure and not clouded by expectations.

The Right Understanding is part of our journey; the path is already beneath our feet. All we have to do is choose to start *and* stay on the path.

Right Understanding is the seed that can grow into a joyful, prosperous life. The other seven practices of the Noble Eightfold Path involve the soil, sunlight, and water that continuously nourish the seed to grow, but we must start with the seed. Make sure you begin with the right seed that you will nourish throughout your life.

Right Understanding of Business

Right Understanding means that when we look at the world with expectations, it is hard to see things as they actually are. Looking at the world with assumptions always clouds our view. Entrepreneurs are notorious for seeing the world through rose-colored glasses. We are wired to believe that our ideas will succeed even in the face of tremendous opposing data. Steve Jobs said it best: "The people who are crazy enough to think they can change the world are the ones who do." It is in our nature to believe we can accomplish anything. Failure is a way to learn and iterate, but it can also mean missed opportunities, layoffs, and catastrophic failure.

When I ran the agency, one of my favorite sayings was "If we have facts, we'll use facts; if we have opinions, we'll just use mine." It wasn't meant to dictate that my view was always correct, and many times, I was utterly wrong. The request was to come to the table with ideas based on data, not on a feeling.

In Annie Duke's book *Thinking in Bets*, she articulates how life and business are very similar to a game of poker. During each individual hand throughout the game, each player tries to make the best possible decision based on the incomplete information they possess. The more information we have to reference, the better our choices will be. And just like in poker, it's possible to make the statistically correct decision yet have an improbable outcome resulting in failure.

The worst trap we can fall into is "resulting bias." Annie argues that we can justify poor decisions if they result in positive outcomes and regret statistically correct choices that result in bad results. It is easier to realize you are suffering from resulting bias in poker than in business because the odds are consistent; however, the situation can change as the hand progresses. Pocket aces is an excellent hand until four cards to a flush are on the board, and you are not holding that suit. Suddenly, what was an 80 percent favorite to win the hand has shifted to being a tremendous underdog or even drawing dead.

Question
How can we tell if we are making the right decision?

Truthful Answer
We can't!

It's impossible to know what the future holds in our business or personal life. What we *can* do is make the best decision possible with the information we have at the time and move forward. It's better to make a decision once you have as much information as possible to avoid analysis paralysis. It's worse for an organization to suffer from a lack of decisions than from the wrong one. This is why the iterative process is so effective in product development. Our teams believe that we understand exactly what our customers want. Still, instead of wasting resources building software or a physical product on a hunch, we start by asking our customers.

Case Study: ibotta

When the founder of this unicorn company first approached my agency to help design the app that would become a multibillion-dollar publicly traded company, we started with paper prototypes sketched on printer paper rather than spending weeks developing the different sections of the application. Why? The idea was good enough to receive a few million dollars in their first round of funding, so it must be great, right? Probably, but why take the risk of designing and developing software when we can validate our hypotheses while gaining insights from our customers' pain points? The first iterations came from whiteboard brainstorming sessions that resulted in low-fidelity sketched prototypes. We sketched out each page of the application with a Sharpie and presented them to our target audience: coupon users. This was an essential step in creating an engaging user experience since neither the founder nor I had ever clipped a coupon in our entire lives. By talking to the target audience about their needs before expending resources (time and money), ibotta went from a basement in downtown Denver with two employees to a publicly traded company worth over two billion dollars.

Another misconception today is the myth of "overnight success." In reality, almost every business that appears to have instant ascension to fame and riches has been working hard for a long, long time. There is the rare anomaly that does explode onto the scene with exponential growth, and due to the visibility of those brands, we are fooled into thinking we should expect that kind of alchemy. What is not seen are the thousands upon thousands of catastrophic business failures that balance the scales of expectations if you look at the data.

The two things required to be successful in business are clarity of vision and discipline.

Clarity of Vision

To consistently achieve results in any organization, we have to have a shared vision that is clear enough to be understood by all. Whether the goal is to cure hunger or to develop the next piece of software to disrupt an industry, you must start with a clear vision of the final destination.

Don't get clarity confused with unhealthy desires that will harm your Karma in pursuit of achieving them. Building a business to make a billion dollars to spend on a luxurious lifestyle while pacifying our ego isn't healthy. Being driven by our desires can cause us to make sacrifices in the parts of our lives that should never be compromised. No business meeting is worth missing a child's birthday or graduation. I have met billionaires who have destroyed their health and broken their families in pursuit of more. When driven by the wrong motivation, finding a balance between work and personal life is impossible. It comes down to sacrifices and consequences.

When a business is positively contributing to the world, whether that's through developing an environmentally friendly laundry detergent, building a better widget, or simply being in an ethical industry that doesn't harm its customers or others in the pursuit of profits, it's completely acceptable to make a salary that reflects the value added to the organization.

To have clarity of vision, an organization must have a clear goal to work toward. We should have aspirations to achieve business success. Goal setting is vital for a multitude of reasons. Pablo Picasso said it best: "Our goals can only be reached through a vehicle of a plan, in which we must fervently believe, and upon which we must vigorously act." Without direction, making meaningful progress is a struggle, and we will fall short of our full potential. But always remember that goals are not about keeping score; they are only meant to have direction (clarity of vision).

Discipline

The second key ingredient in a successful business is discipline. Having the willpower to do the work required is literally the difference between a dream and making it a reality. With discipline, we can execute today what our future selves will be grateful for tomorrow.

There are a few simple tools we can use to improve our discipline:

- Get into the flow state
- MVP approach (minimal viable product)
- Stop starting, start finishing

Flow State.   Flow is the optimal mental state for the best possible performance. When we are in the flow state, the world seems to melt away as we are completely immersed in our area of focus. Utilizing flow state techniques to maximize focus, creativity, and output is the first tool to be mastered. The flow state is what we enter when we are solely focused on the task at hand. It's when we can do our best work and solve complex problems with ease. The flow state is where an Olympic athlete is in when they are competing in their sport or when rock climber Alex Honnold became the first to free solo climb Yosemite's El Capitan's 3,000-foot face. For the Olympic athlete, focus can be the difference between winning the gold medal or going home empty-handed. For climbers, free soloing thousand-foot rock walls without a rope, it's a matter of life and death.

But it's possible for anyone to enter that focused state of flow without such dramatic stakes. With the right tools, anyone can access this superpower multiple times a day. To enter the flow state, we need to remove ourselves from all distractions. This means turning off your email, putting your phone on airplane mode, silencing all other alerts and distractions, and setting a timer for 30 minutes to an hour to focus solely on one task. Allowing ourselves to do deep work and avoid distraction creates an environment that amplifies creativity and innovation.

At Zenman, we practiced a technique called core hours to encourage our team to enter the flow state at the agency. Each member had staggered core hours allocated for them to work distraction-free without interruption for a 60-minute block in the morning and another 60-minute block every afternoon. The team consistently produced higher-quality work in those short windows each day than the other 75 percent of the time, which was open to distraction.

Pro hack: Use an hourglass instead of an alarm to time your core hours. The alarm going off can be jarring and pull you out of the flow state. The hourglass keeps time but also allows you to stay in the flow longer if you are really in the zone.

Recent studies from the Flow Research Collective have shown that practicing two core hour sprints per day with an active recovery afterward can have a fivefold increase in productivity. The process is simple: the evening before, plan out the most important tasks you need to accomplish and prioritize them. As soon as you wake up in the morning, do the minimal required (brush your teeth and drink some water) and jump right into your task list, starting with the first priority. Work nonstop for two hours straight, then stop and do an active recovery for 90 minutes. Active recovery includes things like working out, taking a walk, meditation, eating healthy meals, or taking a steam shower. The research shows that engaging in an active recovery rather than passive (watching TV, scrolling through social media, etc.) has a significantly higher benefit in reenergizing our minds and bodies. After the active recovery, do one more flow state sprint of two hours and finish with a second active recovery. This protocol maximizes our output, creativity, and problem-solving mental capacity while simultaneously maintaining an active lifestyle.

MVP (Minimal Viable Product). There's a concept in software development called the MVP (minimum viable product). This approach means developing the absolute minimum of anything to validate and get feedback from customers before wasting time, money, and resources. This allows for an iterative approach based on actual feedback from your target audience, enabling you to continue building with validation or pivoting based on your customers' needs. We avoid waste and minimize risk by consistently focusing on building the MVP. This gives a business the Right Understanding of their customers.

This applies to building software, physical products, services, and everything beyond. Validate your offer prior to investing in scale by testing the absolute MVP on your target audience. You've heard the concept that there's no such thing as failure, that all failure is data that you can build on. This is true, but if you're going to fail, fail fast. Avoid wasting valuable resources on instinct when it can be validated with data. If your gut is correct and confirmed with the data, there will always be valuable insights gained from the MVP approach.

When your instinct wasn't as perfect as you had originally envisioned, take that feedback and iterate on your product, service, or application with the insights gained. The ability to pivot quickly is one of the factors that give nimble organizations an advantage. Our world is changing so rapidly that initiatives planned for a year from now could be obsolete before they're complete.

MVP does not mean creating a half-assed product or service. It means creating the minimal product or service to the best of your ability to test in the marketplace. It's about cutting out the bells and whistles before building the core functionality.

Stop Starting and Start Finishing. One of the most significant challenges in staying disciplined today is our constant state of distraction. For entrepreneurs, this means more than just being engrossed with the supercomputer in your pocket constantly going off, alerting you of emails, text messages, and customized offers tailored to your shopping preference and the optimal time to engage you. For founders, the constant stream of new ideas creates a jungle of distractions that hinder them from reaching their goals.

We want to keep all of the ideas, but it's essential to finish what we started. Keep a backlog of all of the projects, ideas, and businesses that you want to start, and leverage a system like a Kanban to help you prioritize your backlog and work on only one or two things at a time. (A Kanban is a visual system that uses columns for "work to be done," "work in progress," and "complete.") When we have dozens of projects in process simultaneously, it means all of them will take significantly longer to complete. Imagine the concept of a dozen half-built bridges instead of one complete bridge. As you build one bridge to completion, it allows you to reach your goal. This enables you to gain momentum for building the second and third bridges. Working on a dozen bridges or projects simultaneously is a horrible use of your time.

How to Practice Right Understanding

To practice Right Understanding means to make the conscious choice every moment to look at what is in front of you in the present moment rather than focus on how you want things to be. You must not close your eyes to the current moment. Siddhartha set out to become the Buddha only after seeing the sickness, old age, and death from which he had been sheltered. That clarity started Siddhartha on his path to enlightenment, just as it will provide you with the ability to comprehend the transiency of everything in our lives.

The Middle Path is necessary to practice Right Understanding in business. Many founders and business leaders fall into the trap of sacrificing their personal and family lives to reach their goals. Like engaging in an industry that does not harm the planet or its inhabitants, we must not harm ourselves or our families in pursuit of success. A workaholic justifies their actions by saying they're doing it for the good of their families. Our families do benefit from our business success, and it's possible to cause damage when our priorities are misaligned. Both can be true simultaneously, but at the end of the race, when you look back on how you ran it, would you make the same choices again, or would you prioritize the small things that got pushed aside in the pursuit of winning?

Learn how to see things as they are. Nothing is permanent.

Tool: Challenge One of Your Truths

Think of something that you believe in your heart and head to be true. The professor of my freshman ethics course in college was astounding at intellectual debates. Dr. Jean let us select any topic and which side of the perspective to debate. Her challenge was that anyone who could ethically prove her wrong would get a 4.0 in the class and would not be required to attend class to do any of the assigned work or final exam. I debated with the professor multiple times a week and lost every single time. Her ability to look at any topic from all angles empowered her to see things the rest of us miss.

What is something that you believe to be true?

_____

_____

_____

_____

Why do you have this belief? What data reinforces this hypothesis?

_____

_____

_____

_____

_____

_____

Now, it's time to switch teams. State the opposing view from your original "truth." Take your time before writing it down to clearly articulate the opinion so it can be debated.

_____

_____

_____

_____

(continued)

(*continued*)

How would you convince someone of the opposing view
that you just stated? What data, examples, or arguments
would you make?

_____

_____

_____

_____

_____

_____

_____

_____

_____

_____

_____

*Did you do this with a mind that was open to changing your
view based on new information? How did your perspective
change? Repeat this exercise with a new topic if it didn't.*

CHAPTER

6

Impermanence

In Buddhism, impermanence (a part of Right Understanding in Chapter 5) is a fundamental principle that states that all things are subject to change, decay, and death. Our suffering intensifies when we hold on to temporary circumstances with the hope of making them permanent. All that exists will eventually be no more; nothing lasts forever. It feels overwhelming when we initially grasp that it is inescapable, but accepting it can also be liberating. Regardless of your perspective, it is an inevitable fact of life. All things are intrinsically subject to change.

The Stoics also embraced this concept. Seneca said, "Let us prepare our minds as if we'd come to the very end of life. Let us postpone nothing. Let us balance life's books each day. The one who puts the finishing touches on their life each day is never short of time."

Acquiring this kind of awareness commands reflection. Through meditation and contemplation, we come to accept the reality of the transitoriness of all things, integrating it into our wisdom. It allows us to focus on what really matters in life and stop wasting time on the things that don't.

Heraclitus said, "No man ever steps in the same river twice, for it's not the same river, and he's not the same man." He meant that we are constantly growing and evolving, as is the world around us. The man is not the same because he's learned from his experiences, hardships, and triumphs. The river is not the same because it changes with the seasons. From the life in the river to the water flowing, both are entirely different.

Think about it on a cellular level. The very cells that make up our bodies are continuously dying and being replaced by new ones from before our birth, right up until we take our last breath. Even our own bodies are constantly changing from moment to moment. This continuous evolution of ourselves and circumstances in the world around us isn't always a bad thing. Many times in life, change is welcome and embraced.

"This too shall pass" also applies to times when we face challenges in our lives. The pain we feel at the end of a relationship or the loss of a loved one is acute at first; the hurt can be unbearable. However, in time, this pain will gradually lessen and pass. Buddha declared that nothing in the world is fixed or permanent. Everything in this world is subject to change, but it doesn't have to be for the worse.

Practicing nonattachment (Anatta and Anicca) liberates us by teaching that phenomena are impermanent (Annica), and nonself (Anatta) allows the letting go of attachments to outcomes, which eliminates past regrets and worry about the future.

Impermanence in Business

Understanding impermanence is the starting point to enlightenment in our personal lives and an essential concept to master in business. If we look at some of the business giants over the last several decades that have entirely disappeared, it's painfully apparent just how quickly the landscape can change. A brand or even an industry can become completely obsolete in an incredibly short window of time. This goes beyond bad choices in a changing landscape that led to industry leaders disappearing altogether, such as Blockbuster and BlackBerry not responding to disruptions to the market. Instead of embracing that change was upon them, both companies failed to see the risk until it was too late.

Other businesses didn't have the opportunity to pivot. From photographic film processing labs and video stores to encyclopedias and the Yellow Pages, some industries that existed for decades or centuries went extinct in a very short time. It's easy to understand in retrospect how the leaders of those companies should have seen the writing on the wall and pivoted by investing in emerging technologies, but most lacked the expertise and/or resources to make that quantum leap. It's hard to imagine that a technology or change in how customers consume a product or service can completely change an industry before it happens. Taxi drivers never feared losing the lion's share of their customers to complete strangers driving their own personal cars.

The Covid pandemic of 2020 is an excellent example of how control is only an illusion. Nobody was prepared for a global shutdown that changed how humans shopped, dined, and interacted for two years. Everything from retail and hospitality to commercial real estate changed forever. Suddenly, our groceries were being delivered along with duck confit for dinner simultaneously, while we learned that some businesses no longer needed office space and could increase productivity and profit by utilizing technology, structure, and strategic in-person connection.

Embracing Impermanence

How do we embrace impermanence in business? We must accept that even if we do the right thing and work hard, the end result can be filled with heartbreak and disappointment. That can actually be an incredibly liberating mindset. Understanding that we can do our best and still fail, but deciding to move forward anyway, creates the perfect conditions for accomplishing extraordinary feats.

In building an agency, we had to work our way up from "C" and "D" clients to our "A" and "B" clients. "D" Clients would be underfunded first-time founders who would call asking for us to build a combination of Amazon and Facebook for $2,500. These customers didn't understand the scope of what they wanted to build creating delusions of grandeur. "C" clients would typically be small businesses bootstrapping as they scaled, usually without experience in the digital marketplace. When we finally graduated to working with somebody who had a budget that wasn't coming directly from a checking account they were personally associated with, it was considered a "B" client. This meant things like "change requests" and "maintenance contracts" existed in their vocabulary.

I spent over a decade working with small businesses and challenging inexperienced leaders before I got my first shot at an enterprise project. In my case, when it rained, it poured. My agency's first two six-figure projects came at the same time. It was the most exciting week in my professional career, although I had no idea it would turn into a nightmare less than a month later. These projects required resources Zenman didn't have on staff, so we outsourced some of the development to a strategic partner. What I didn't know and could never have predicted was that this so-called strategic partner would immediately shut down the business that was under contract with Zenman to complete the backend development work on both projects. The person that I had just paid over $100,000 as the 50 percent deposit on their development work tried to go behind my back to both clients to get Zenman out of the projects entirely. They even convinced one of the clients to try to get Zenman to pay them for the work due to a loophole in the contract's errors and emissions clause.

Talk about impermanence. I went from doubling the agency's revenue to panic attacks, losing 30 pounds, working with a therapist to deal with extreme stress, and wasting over $100,000 in legal fees to be able to part ways with the contractor and one of the two clients. To add insult to injury, the client was actually the one in breach of our contract for soliciting/hiring our subcontractors. We had been 100 percent in the right both ethically and contractually, but that one mistake almost put my company out of business. Even worse, our first time up to the plate in the big leagues, we not only struck out, we ended up in litigation. Would we ever get another chance to work with clients at that scale again? No, the clients we ended up working with far exceeded them! Before selling Zenman, we had created the websites for Frontier Airlines (there are only so many airlines, and we got selected out of hundreds of agencies in the RFP process), RE/ MAX (the largest real estate company in the world), the Lumineers, American Express, and many other global giants.

We never know what the future holds or when not getting what we want is actually the most significant gift we can receive. Sometimes it's hard to see that in the moment, but know that everything is happening exactly how it's supposed to unfold.

As the Buddha said, "Do not dwell in the past, do not dream of the future, concentrate the mind on the present moment."

Tool: This, Too, Shall Pass

The one constant is that whatever we are experiencing right now will eventually cease to exist. Whether we are in good times or facing the most challenging parts of our lives, with time, this too shall come to pass. Our lives are precious and fleeting, spanning a blink of an eye when compared to all of existence.

Imagine that today would be the last day of your life. Describe how you would spend your time today, knowing you only had 24 hours left. Thinking about our death encourages us to repair relationships and forgive others. It also puts into perspective how we spend each day, giving us clarity on how we should spend each precious minute of this gift called life.

_____

_____

_____

_____

_____

_____

_____

_____

_____

_____

_____

_____

_____

_____

_____

_____

(continued)

(*continued*)

_____

_____

_____

_____

_____

_____

_____

_____

_____

_____

_____

_____

_____

_____

_____

_____

_____

_____

_____

_____

_____

_____

_____

_____

7

Wabi-Sabi (侘び寂び)

Wabi-sabi is a Japanese concept that encourages finding beauty in the imperfect and impermanent. When we are bombarded with a fast-paced lifestyle and worldly desires, we are constantly shown what perfection looks like in publications, billboards, and films. It's understandable that we've become obsessed with perfection. The pressures of society and social media compound misinforming us to strive for the unachievable.

Wabi-sabi helps us find beauty in the imperfect, reminding us that all things, including ourselves, are imperfect. Knowing that all things in life are in an imperfect, constant state of change (decay), we must strive for excellence, not perfection. When our goal is unattainable, it will block our creativity and limit our ability to reach our full potential in business and in life.

Three Fundamental Principles of Wabi-Sabi

Right Understanding (see Chapter 5) teaches us to accept impermanence. Wabi-sabi helps us embrace the imperfect and see beauty in the flawed and temporary. The roots date back to 15th-century Japan, when a Zen monk broke with the tradition of using ornate utensils in his tea ceremony and replaced them with simple ones. There is an elegant and simple beauty in wabi-sabi that follows the three fundamental principles: Acceptance of Imperfection, Appreciation of Transience, and Connection to Nature.

Acceptance of Imperfection

The first principle is to accept that both ourselves and the world we live in are imperfect. By embracing flaws and deficiencies, we can find beauty rather than inferiority. The embrace of imperfection allows us to appreciate the person, object, or moment we are experiencing in the present moment.

This acceptance is becoming continuously more challenging in modern society. From the ads using models edited to remove even the slightest flaws to the filters everyday people apply to photos on social media that magically eliminate imperfections, society is conditioning us to the pursuit of the impossible. There is so much more beauty in the real world than the digitally manipulated online versions; embrace reality and spend more time being present.

In business, perfect can be the enemy of done. Seeking perfection is also counterproductive to the MVP (minimal viable product) approach. While I would never advocate releasing a product or service before it's ready, I would plead with you to know when it's time to share your creation with the world. One of the best examples of this in the business world was

Microsoft versus Apple in the race for personal computers. Bill Gates famously released the Windows operating system and tools before Steve Jobs introduced Macintosh. Other factors like cost and software selection factored into Microsoft's dominance for decades in the business landscape, with mostly only creatives embracing Macintosh, but the keystone of Gates's success was being first.

Appreciation of Transience

The second principle is embracing the transience or vanishing nature of life. Nothing is permanent in life. Every one of us was born; we will grow and die someday. This cycle is essential to appreciating the magnificence and the miracle of life. Our understanding of fleetingness allows us to be present and to relish each moment. By not holding on to regrets from our past or worrying about the future, we let go of our expectations and our craving to fulfill them.

We are a collection of atoms on a rock circling a star that's billions of years old hurtling through space. Our very existence is a blink of an eye, and if we fail to embrace the transience of that truth, life will be a struggle we cannot win.

Connection to Nature

The third and final principle is to nurture our connection with nature. Wabi-sabi shows us that nature is the ultimate source of quintessence. The fractal patterns and Fibonacci structures that appear repeatedly in the natural world have a significant impact on our physical and mental well-being. (Chapter 14 has more information on Shinrin Yoku, or "Forest Bathing," and the benefits of spending time in nature.)

Our mind's neurotransmitters have evolved to keep us alive. Through our fight or flight responses, our brain releases cortisol when we feel in danger, which helped keep our ancient ancestors alive. When they sensed that there might be a saber-toothed tiger, their hypothalamus and pituitary gland in the brain released cortisol, their adrenal glands released adrenaline, and they could run further and faster to stay alive. The problem is that our brains have not evolved as quickly as our society has. We no longer experience the kind of threats that our ancestors lived through, but the same cortisol and adrenaline are released into our bodies when we're stopped by a red light on the way to a meeting or get an angry voicemail from a client. The business and personal challenges that cause our brains to react are not life-threatening, but our bodies can't tell the difference, and to exacerbate this, most of us are removed from the pressure release valve our minds have had for thousands of years. That release is being in nature. Seeing the fractal patterns in nature triggers a physiological response that reduces cortisol.

Wabi-Sabi in Business

If we only attempt what we know we will do perfectly, our best ideas will end up in the cemetery with us, unrealized and lost forever. When we understand that our efforts will not result in perfection, we can get busy working toward building something excellent. This lends itself to the Lean Product Development approach in building anything from software to automobiles.

This approach is how Team Wikispeed built a fast, affordable, ultra-efficient, safe, fun commuter car that gets over 100 mpg in three short months. They used the Agile methodology, running seven-day sprints to make changes as quickly as they learned along the way. The car's chassis is the lightest ever built to receive a five-star crash rate equivalency, and it was achieved by building tests for components before they ever built the chassis taken from the test-driven software development methodology.

How is this possible? By clearly defining the objective and then breaking it down into bite-sized pieces. In Agile software development, those bite-sized pieces are called user stories, and those user stories are weighted by points, which equate to level of effort and include a clearly defined definition of acceptance. The user stories are then prioritized in a backlog that informs the order in which they should be completed. Each team member has only one or two user stories in development at any given time. Once the item is finished, it's moved from "work in progress" to "done." The most important secret to the success of Agile development is that we build the MVP, avoiding adding bells and whistles that are not valuable to the end result.

The opposite approach is to wait until something is perfect before releasing it. The textbook example of this are the 15 websites I built for my digital agency, Zenman, over 23 years. Of the 15 websites we spent hundreds of hours and countless dollars designing and developing, only nine saw the light of day. The other six spent months, then years, being refined, tweaked, and massaged until they were obsolete, and we would start entirely over with the next iteration. I guarantee each of those sites would have generated millions in new client revenue if we had abandoned our quest for perfection and accepted excellence as "good enough."

Monks in northern Japan have been participating in a yearly ritual since the eighth century, seeking enlightenment of their mind, body, and soul. Their core philosophy can be distilled down to one word—*Uketamo*, which means "I humbly accept with an open heart." It refers to complete acceptance of both the wonderful and challenging experiences throughout life.

How liberating is it to accept the outcome regardless of whether we perceive it as good or bad? As long as we have done our best in pursuit of excellence, we can release attachment to the result. If we continue to resist, we will continue to compound our suffering.

Tool: Release Our Ego and Accept Imperfection

Do you know where the most valuable real estate in the world is? You might think it's in Manhattan or maybe someplace on the beach in Santa Barbara, but the most valuable real estate in the world is in the cemetery. Why? Because of all of the businesses that didn't get started, the songs that didn't get written, and the other creative endeavors someone was afraid to embark on for fear of it not being enough. There's a simple exercise you can do every day to unblock your ego and tap into the most creative parts of your subconscious. It entails free flow stream-of-consciousness writing for at least 10 minutes or two pages to start each day.

Write for 10 minutes to unblock your ego. Take this practice into your daily life and start every day with this creative exercise, and you will be amazed at the ideas that arise from within.

_____

_____

_____

_____

_____

_____

_____

_____

_____

_____

_____

_____

8

Right Thought

Right Thought is having clarity of vision. It's continuously cultivating positive states of mind like empathy, compassion, and love while avoiding negative thoughts like envy, hatred, and jealousy. Right Thought requires we start with the Right Understanding (see Chapter 5), which is the overarching principle that informs thought, speech, action, livelihood, effort, mindfulness, and concentration.

Every thought we have is planting a seed in our mind that will eventually grow into whatever flower or weed we create. It all starts with the right impression, the right seed. We've all heard the saying "Whether you believe you can or you believe you can't—you're right." This thought will eventually become a reality, so don't create a future you fear. Think about the future in a positive way and align your energy with it.

Visualization works for this very reason. When we free our minds of limiting beliefs and fear of the worst possible outcome, it allows us to align our thoughts and energy with the pure objective.

The Three Stages of Right Thought

There are three stages to Right Thought, beginning with awareness of negative or evil thoughts, releasing those thoughts, and the intentional cultivation of pure thoughts:

1. Becoming aware of our thought process
2. Letting go of negative thoughts and patterns
3. Cultivating goodwill

Becoming Aware of Our Thought Process

We start by becoming aware of our thoughts, and analyze them to see if they are helping to attract the best results. Try to identify thoughts and emotions that form a pattern and label them. For example, if you frequently think, "I am not smart enough to (fill-in-the-blank)" or "I don't know how to solve that problem," those are similar beliefs around "not intelligent," which is a tremendously limiting belief. One of the predominant self-fulfilling prophecies is "I am not creative." This truly breaks my heart because I believe everyone is creative, but after childhood the fear of judgment robs us of the confidence to do innovative things.

As you become aware of each thought, examine it through these lenses:

- Is this thought kind?
- Does this thought benefit me?
- Does this thought benefit others?

Treat your thoughts the same way Grandma told you to treat your words: "If you can't say anything nice, don't say anything at all." This is exactly the same idea, but with thoughts. Why would you hold ill will or hatred toward someone? If you have negative thoughts about someone else or yourself, become aware of them.

Letting Go of Negative Thoughts

Once we are conscious of our thought process, we can let go of negative thoughts and patterns. When thoughts arise in our minds, we can choose to engage in them or simply let them pass if they do not serve us.

Thoughts have the power to take us from the present moment. Even when we are experiencing pure bliss, our minds can wander from the present to worrying about how soon it will be over or how to possibly extend it rather than enjoying it right now. How many people do you see at concerts holding up their phones and recording a video? They are missing the magic of the moment that can never be experienced through a video, no matter how many "likes" it gets on social media.

By living in the present, we can choose to reframe or release negative thoughts as we experience them in real time. Focusing on the past or future only intensifies the thoughts and patterns we need to let go of. The past can't be changed, and the only way to influence the future is through our actions in the present. When those negative thoughts enter our mind, acknowledge them and choose to consciously release them.

Cultivating Goodwill

It's possible to cultivate a mind that does not engage in evil thoughts, but it's unrealistic to try to achieve a state where we never start to have negative thoughts. The key is when we realize that a jealous or otherwise evil thought is entering our consciousness, we choose not to engage. I like to take it one step further and turn any thought that starts out unpure into an authentic appreciation or positive affirmation.

Suppose I see someone driving a Ferrari who looks like he is 23 and couldn't hold a job as a barista for more than a week. In that case, my first thought might be, "Look at that trust fund kid; there is no way he earned that." But when I recognize that envy, I immediately shift to a thought like "Wow, I wonder what incredible creative or innovative thing they must have created or accomplished to have the freedom to dress that casually and to afford such a beautiful car." Once we recognize the negative thought, it's simple to mindfully shift our perspective to a positive one. In every situation, try to assume positive intent; we never know what the other person is experiencing and the challenges they might be facing.

With our minds, we make the world. Speak or act with kindness, and happiness will follow you as surely as a shadow follows the person who casts it.

—Buddhist Philosophy

Right Thought in Business

Where our thoughts go, our energy flows. Whatever our mind is focused on will eventually become our reality. This could be accomplishing this quarter's business goals, finding the right relationship partner, or if we aren't practicing Right Thought and are focusing on thoughts of scarcity rather than abundance, we can actually manifest a crisis. We need to focus on the life we want to live, not the things we fear. It is not my perspective that we should be constantly trying to achieve unrealistic growth or unachievable goals in business and life. But I do believe we need to play to win rather than playing not to lose. In many sports, a good defense is an excellent offense. In life and in business, we want to play to win.

The Law of Attraction

Like attracts like, which summarizes the law of attraction. It's long been believed that when we have an abundance mindset, the result will be good fortune, but if we suffer from a scarcity mindset, it will manifest hardship. We have seen this play out over and over in our personal lives and businesses, and now science is studying this phenomenon.

String theory attempts to merge quantum mechanics with Einstein's theory of relativity. In this theory, point-like particles are replaced with strings. These strings are constantly vibrating, and the frequency of that vibration changes. Understanding that like attracts like, it makes sense that we project into the world to attract back the same frequency. Many scientists theorize that these strings' vibrations are subconscious awareness.

> *"Laistrygonians, Cyclops, angry Poseidon—don't be afraid of them;
> . . . you won't encounter them unless you bring them along inside your
> soul, unless your soul sets them up in front of you."*
> —From the poem Ithaka *by C.P. Cavafy*

Successful leaders can use the Law of Attraction to achieve business objectives, and the same principles are true in our personal lives. The first and most important step is clearly defining what you want to attract. Almost every business methodology includes setting our long-term vision and most include a stretch goal or BHAG (Big Hairy Audacious Goal). The simple act of writing down our goals doubles the probability of reaching it.

The Power of Visualization

In the 1950s, the University of Chicago conducted a study to see how visualization could have a positive impact on their athletes' performance. The study was conducted on a group of basketball players broken into three segments. The first segment was told to spend an hour a day practicing their free throws, the second segment was asked to visualize themselves making free throws every day for an hour without actually taking a shot, and the third segment was told to do nothing.

As you can imagine, the segment that neither did visualization or practice showed no improvement. The first segment that practiced an hour a day saw a 24 percent improvement in their free throw percentage. The second segment that was asked to visualize shooting free throws for an hour a day without touching a basketball saw a 23 percent improvement in their free throw shooting percentage. This is only 1 percent less than the group that spent an hour a day practicing free throws.

Steve Jobs utilized visualization to ideate Apple's most innovative products. He frequently came up with ideas that his engineers said were impossible, but he would tell them to "figure it out." Jobs said, "I'm convinced that about half of what separates successful entrepreneurs from the non-successful ones is pure perseverance."

I can also give you an example of wrong thought. There were times early in my career when the agency was struggling, and rather than invest in planting seeds of positivity that I could nurture, I would Google other agencies that I knew were experiencing worse challenges in a sick way of self-medicating through shared suffering rather than facing my problems head on. I needed to be a bison. Bison are incredible animals. The bison turns and marches head-first into the blizzard when it sees an approaching storm. Other animals huddle together, awaiting the approaching storm and waiting for it to pass. The bison spends less time suffering because it faces challenges head on and marches straight through them.

"I am" are the two most powerful words in existence. When we state "I am," it's a declaration to the universe that is listening and will deliver. That is why it's crucial that we intentionally use our Right Thoughts. If our thoughts are limiting or negative, that will be what we manifest in the future. There is no reason to worry about worst-case scenarios that will create challenges in the future. Enjoy the present moment and plant seeds that are courageous, challenging, and pure.

Company Vision

A long-term goal that is clearly articulated is like a vision board for your business. Putting your 10-year goal down on paper puts energy in motion. About 40 percent of US adults make New Year's resolutions, yet only around 3 percent of the world's population write down their goals, even though we know that writing down our goals increases the chances of them coming to fruition by almost double (43 percent). Most New Year resolutions have been abandoned by February, and over 90 percent will fail to keep the resolution.

Writing down a clearly stated goal boosts the probability of success exponentially to the point that it should be done every week. State your goal and track how far along you are in reaching it weekly. This informs what is the most important to do next. If the goal is something like "Quarterly Sales Quota," that isn't an actionable step. That needs to be broken down into monthly, weekly, and daily tasks that will all together combine to achieving the goal—daily calls with warm leads, for example, with a weekly newsletter and monthly webinars would be actionable steps toward the bigger goals. None of that is possible without a clear vision for the organization to work toward.

Tool: Future Press Release

Our thoughts and words create impressions in our minds like seeds that will eventually grow. We want to plant seeds of fruit and flour, not weeds. Your thoughts matter tremendously in creating the future you will ultimately live with. Let's plant a seed for a future beyond your wildest expectations. Write a press release for a significant event five years from today. It could be a business achievement like an acquisition, making a scientific breakthrough and receiving the Nobel Prize, or your daughter winning an Olympic gold medal.

Note: Don't mistake having direction for unhealthy desire. How we pursue our dreams is the difference between an unhealthy thirst to feed our ego and material goals and having clarity of direction so we can have our impact on the world.

Future Date (five years from today)

_____

Headline:

_____
_____
_____

Three key highlights from the story:

_____
_____
_____
_____
_____

_____

_____

A quote from you about the story:

_____

_____

_____

_____

_____

_____

9

Being Present (Sati)

By practicing Sati ((स्)ति, which translates to "awareness" or "mindfulness"), we live in the present moment by paying close attention to our thoughts, feelings, and sensations without judgment. Being consciously present makes it possible to create a state of Right Thought (see Chapter 8). Sati is followed with Sampanjañña, which is "clear comprehension." This means being aware mindfully in the present moment and clearly comprehending what is happening with our body and mind.

In the past, it was easier to train our minds, but this has become tremendously more challenging due to the distractions of modern society. The technology that was meant to make our lives easier continuously interrupts us with alerts from emails, messages, and news. In a world where you can get anything from groceries to a new car delivered to your doorstep in hours if not minutes, society has become accustomed to an on-demand expectation. We are *not* meant to be tethered to a device and forced to react every time it chimes.

To be present today, a mindfulness practice is essential. Mindfulness trains you to become aware of what's happening in your body and mind, along with the world around you. Meditation will help with being present at that moment during your day, but we need to consciously make an effort to be present for the remaining parts of the day.

Releasing the Past

If you are depressed, you are living in the past. If you are anxious, you are living in the future. If you are at peace, you are living in the present.

—*Lao Tzu*

To be fully present, we must not be living in the past or fantasizing about the future. When we spend our time focused on past regrets, it creates suffering for no reason. If our energy is spent focusing on dreams of the future rather than experiencing this moment in time, we miss the most precious and decisive moments. This doesn't mean we completely ignore history. If lessons from the past are forgotten or ignored, those challenges are destined to repeat themselves until the end of time. We learn from our past experiences, successes, and failures without focusing our energy on things that we can't change or things that have yet to come to pass.

Focusing on the past fosters discontentment if we are unhappy about how a chapter of our life has unfolded. Replaying past experiences and contemplating how we could have reacted or approached a particular situation in our past does not serve us. It is essential to learn from our experiences. It's powerful if we can share our experiences with others so they can avoid stepping into the same potholes we did. Life is too short to learn everything from our own experiences, and if we can learn through observation and shared experience, we can avoid some of those mistakes that have already been made historically.

The past is behind us, and no amount of contemplation can change anything that has already come to pass. Rather than look at the challenges we've faced or even the trauma we've experienced with resentment, it doesn't serve. Understand that everything we've experienced has prepared us for exactly where we are today. Our past does not define us, and when we release it, there is space created to focus on today. If you see any failure as data in your learning, it is not a bad thing. Thomas Edison once said, "I have not failed 10,000 times; I've successfully found 10,000 ways that will not work."

Another equally dangerous way to dream about the past is contemplating those "better years" at an earlier time in life. It is nice to think about the glorious experiences that we've had throughout life, but we also tend to remember only the good things. Living in the past means missing out on the present. If this isn't the best moment of your life, it means one of two things. First, it could be that right now you're facing one of the challenges meant to help you grow and learn the lessons in this life that are essential to your growth. It could also mean that you've been neglecting aspects of your personal or business life. Both of these situations can be resolved to make the present a profoundly beautiful time. In fact, sometimes all it takes is being present and taking a walk in nature to understand that right now is the greatest gift we could possibly hope for.

Not fantasizing about the future does not mean we don't have a clear direction. Sometimes, we have to rely on our instincts to help us find the right path. In his book *The Lion Tracker's Guide to Life*, Boyd Varty says, "I may not know where I am going, but I know how to get there."

Technology Distractions

Our phones have turned humans into the most distracted species on planet Earth. Most people wake up in the morning with the alarm on their phone going off and immediately start looking at text messages, email, or, worse, social media. The first 10 minutes after we wake up and the last 10 minutes before we fall asleep is a magical time to hack our subconscious. The last thing anyone needs to do right before drifting off to sleep is reading client emails or scrolling through today's breaking news. We are not meant to be tethered to and constantly distracted by the super-computer in our pocket.

The blue light that's emitted by our devices inhibits our brain's ability to release melatonin, which we need in our circadian rhythm. Many devices have the ability to filter out that blue light, but it does not change the fact that your brain processes billions of pixels every second. Netflix and chill is an oxymoron. There is a reason binge-watching is such an epidemic. Every time you hit the next episode or your thumb scrolls to the next screen on social media, your brain releases a little bit of dopamine. This is the same neurotransmitter released when someone snorts cocaine.

The best thing you can do for your mental health and physical well-being is to stay off screens for at least 30 minutes or an hour, if possible, after you wake up and for 30 minutes or an hour before you fall asleep. Read a book, meditate, and play games with your loved ones, but don't reply to emails or browse the web.

Our brains need downtime to innovate and be creative. You have a technology addiction if you can't sit through a stoplight without pulling out your phone. Many of the ideas that have shaped the world we live in today came to those inventors when they had time to contemplate undistracted and uninterrupted.

Our phones also disengage us from those around us. When you are on your cellphone, distracted by the human sitting across the table from you, it speaks volumes about what's actually important to you. You're saying, "Staying tethered to whatever has my attention is more important to me than the time we have together right now." On rare occasions, there's actually a situation that justifies interrupting an in-person connection with a digital device, so have the common courtesy to excuse yourself and speak in private. Don't have the other person suffer the humiliation of waiting while you focus on the toy in your hand. Just having our phones on the table has been shown to distract us from being present. The sheer presence of a phone, even if it's facedown, is a mental distraction that subconsciously takes your attention, reducing your focus and cognitive capacity. Our brains have been trained to be expecting a notification so we are actively distracted with the urge to check our alerts.

The two practices I use to be present throughout the day are limiting the times that I communicate via email and turning my cellphone on silent/do not disturb for most of the day. Of course, I have my kids, family, and an extremely short list of my closest friends configured to be able to reach me anytime, but when it comes to literally anyone else, unless there is a scheduled call, I don't interrupt my flow anytime the phone rings to answer it. My work is not a life and death responsibility, and unless your job is one in which people's lives depend on a real-time response, nothing is so important that it requires dropping everything to respond to.

Pro Hack: 3-2-1-Zero Email. Schedule the time to respond to emails. The 3-2-1-Zero is a technique where you look at and respond to email for 30 minutes, twice a day, read every email only once, and get your inbox down to zero. Your inbox is the least efficient to-do list possible and marking an email "unread" after reading it is a tremendous waste of time and brain power by literally doubling the effort. The only way to overcome this is via email hygiene. If you can unsubscribe from a list, don't just delete the email—unsubscribe once and for all. We are not meant to spend the majority of our day staring at screens responding to email. It is possible to do all of your communications in one hour if you are disciplined. Parkinson's Law is the concept that work expands to fill the time we allocate to accomplish it. If we leave a task deadline open ended, it will take forever to complete, but if we allocate a limited amount of time for a task (like email), we can complete it in that time.

(I understand that if you have a thousand emails a day, this is not feasible. My point is that you do *not* need to receive a thousand emails a day. Remove yourself from the extraneous communication to keep only what is essential, and give yourself the time to actually respond to the communications that require your input and genius.)

The Tiger and the Strawberry

There is an ancient Zen parable that tells the story of a monk, a tiger, and a strawberry. It helps us look at life, and in particular the present moment, from an awakened perspective.

One day, a monk was traveling down a path, and he encountered a man-eating tiger. The monk slowly backed away, and the tiger followed him, growling as he approached. Walking backward, the monk went off the path and found himself at the edge of a cliff. As the tiger was almost upon him, he looked down and saw a lone vine. The monk grabbed hold of the vine and began descending the cliff as the hungry tiger growled at him from above. Trembling, the monk began to climb down the vine when he looked down only to see that below, two tigers paced, waiting to make him their dinner. Only the vine sustained him. At that moment, two mice, one white and one black, emerged from a crack and started to gnaw away at the vine little by little—the only thing keeping him alive. At that moment, he noticed a ripe strawberry growing close to where he hung. The monk plucked the strawberry and took a bite. It was the most delicious flavor.

My understanding of this Zen fable is that the white mouse represents the future, and the black mouse represents the past. Both are chewing away at the vine the monk clung to for dear life when he notices the strawberry, which I believe represents the present. Oh, how sweet it tastes when we live in the now.

> *The secret of health for both mind and body is not to mourn for the past, worry about the future, or anticipate troubles, but to lie in the present moment wisely and earnestly.*
>
> *—Buddha*

Sati in Business

Practicing Sati, or mindfulness, in the business setting will profoundly benefit your employees' mental health, relationships, and performance in their roles. The results are so significant and consistent that some of the world's leading organizations, such as Apple, Oprah, Nike, and Google, have incorporated mindfulness into the workplace.

The benefits of mindfulness in business setting include:

- Stress reduction
- Increase in output
- Reduction in workplace conflict
- Enhanced creativity
- Improved cognitive performance
- Happier employees (improved morale)

Sadly, many organizations misunderstand mindfulness as distracting employees' focus or negatively impacting culture, when nothing could be further from the truth. A mindfulness practice, especially in a group setting, will significantly increase productivity. A recent study by Aetna showed that employees who participated in a single mindfulness activity gained over an hour of productivity as a result. At first it might seem counterintuitive that taking time to clear our minds and sit in silence will equal more work completed at a higher rate of accuracy and innovation, but study after study reinforces this truth. Happier, healthier employees consistently outperform their overworked and burnt-out counterparts.

The same technology distractions that keep us from being present in our personal lives are magnified in the business environment. It's become acceptable for meetings to have participants in various states of distraction on laptops or phones taking their focus away from the topic currently being discussed. Whenever possible, go tech free in the conference room. Remove the screen between participants and take notes with a pen and paper or whiteboard.

Tool: Practicing Presence in Our Day-to-Day Life

With the world at our fingertips (and in our pockets) at all times, we struggle with a plague of constant distraction. How many of you can't sit through a stoplight in traffic without picking up your phone and looking at email or social media? To be present, we must free ourselves from the unhealthy patterns that have been created through convenience and constant access. Create your ideal morning and evening routines that will set you up for success each day. Plan out time for your mindfulness and any other essential self-care, learning, or activity you wish to accomplish each day.

Morning Routine: What are your rituals before looking at technology? Do you use meditation, walking, or some other approach?

_____

_____

_____

_____

_____

_____

Technology Boundaries: Throughout your day, set boundaries and stick to them.

_____

_____

_____

_____

_____

Evening Routine: What is your process for winding down your day (time without screens, meditation, etc.)?

_____

_____

_____

_____

_____

_____

3

Morality (*sila*)

"As a bee gathering nectar does not harm or disturb the color and fragrance of the flower, so do the wise move through the world."

—Buddha

10

Right Speech

M any of us got our first introduction to Right Speech from our grandmother in the form of "If you can't say anything nice, don't say anything at all." Buddhism breaks Right Speech into four elements: lying, idle chatter, divisive or slanderous speech, and abusive speech. The five guidelines for Right Speech are as follows: It is timely, true, gentle, beneficial, and spoken from a place of good intention.

A Few Principles and Tools of Right Speech

Buddha explained Right Speech as only speaking what is true and never saying something that does not have benefit. If we are moved to speak negatively or lie, we need to take that as a signal to look internally at what we are dealing with that could be the root cause, reflect, and intentionally shift our awareness back to a place of mindfulness. Our speech can be an accurate representation of our true thoughts.

In Italian, the phrase *In vino veritas* translates to "In wine there is truth." When someone is under the influence of alcohol, they are likely to let down their guard and tend to share their true feelings, even if it's not really true, gentle, beneficial, and from a place of good intention. Unfortunately, words and actions can never be taken back. We can apologize and make amends, but it doesn't change history or erase them from memory.

Timing Right Speech

Beyond making sure what we say is valuable, we must still be mindful, out of compassion, for the correct time to say it. In business, this translates in the simplest form to "praise in public and criticize in private."

This means that you may wait to speak at times. Avoiding correcting someone in public is an excellent example of when you should not talk. It's hard at times not to interrupt or correct someone when we have different facts or opinions, but ask yourself, "Is this kind?" and "Is this helpful?" At times we choose not to speak up because it could impact someone else by correcting them or contradicting their opinions. This doesn't mean you should stay silent and not have a voice. A good rule of thumb is to speak 20 percent of the time and listen 80 percent of the time. When we are listening, we are learning; when we are talking, we're simply restating what we've heard in the past or our personal opinions. There is a more significant opportunity to grow by listening more than when we are speaking.

I adopted the three-second pause years ago. I read about it in a *Wired* magazine article in the early 2000s, which shared the importance of actually pausing before beginning to speak in a conversation. This does a few things. First, it allows us to truly process what we say before the words leave our mouths. There is no way to take back something once it has been said. This also gives the impression that we authentically listen to the other person. Most conversations have a break in talking of only nanoseconds before the silence is interrupted by someone else speaking. Almost everyone in a conversation is waiting for their opportunity to speak rather than actually listening. The more intelligent individuals tend to talk less and listen more.

The Power of Being Kind

Other times, it means using Right Speech at the right time. When is there an opportunity to say something kind that might improve someone's day? Words or even just a smile can have a life-changing impact on someone. In 2003, the *New Yorker* published an article called "Jumpers" about the overwhelming number of suicides that occur from people jumping off the Golden Gate Bridge. The article ends with the story of a man who had taken his own life by jumping off the bridge, and the medical examiner revealed, "The guy was in his thirties, lived alone, pretty bare apartment. He'd written a note and left it on his bureau. It said, 'I'm going to walk to the bridge. If one person smiles at me on the way, I will not jump.'" It takes almost no effort to be kind, and we never know when a warm smile or friendly "hello" might have a profound impact.

The absence of evil talk (gossip or lies) is a core component of Right Speech. Knowing when to speak is essential, but knowing when *not* to is also a profound skill we should all cultivate. If you are talking about someone, think about how comfortable you would be having this conversation with them in the room.

My personal rule of thumb is that I won't say or put anything in an email or text about someone that I don't feel comfortable speaking in front of that person. Speech is powerful. Our words shape our minds and influence those around us.

Some Tools for Right Speech

I use two tools to communicate effectively. The first tool is a simple question: "What I heard you say was..." This simple recap of what we heard said does multiple things to amplify the effectiveness of your communication. First, it illustrates that you have been listening. Second, it allows us to clarify any misunderstandings. It is consistently mind-blowing when this simple step is used to see how different we hear what was spoken to us. Whether it is from distraction, hearing what we want to hear, or the person speaking struggling to articulate their message, more times than not, we benefit from clarifying.

After you have perfected "What I heard you say was..." and the person speaking confirms it's accurate, move on to the second tool and ask, "Is there more?" Most people just wait for a brief enough pause in the conversation so they can start speaking, which means they aren't authentically listening. Clarifying what you heard the other person say and then asking them to continue ensures the entirety of the message was communicated.

Do you know what the most powerful word in any language is? It's the name of the person you're speaking to. When communicating with somebody, make the effort to know their name. Even if it's the clerk at a gas station or the barista at the coffee shop this morning, read the name on their name tag and say, "Good morning, Jordan." Or if it's a hipster coffee shop and the dress code is bell bottoms rather than name tags, ask what their name is, introduce yourself, and thank them by name. Never forget that a person's name is the most important word in any language to them.

The most overlooked form of communication is actually nonverbal. It's estimated that at least 70 percent and as high as 93 percent of all communication is nonverbal. A tenet called the 7-38-55 rule is a concept that breaks down how we communicate. Only 7 percent of communication is through the words we speak, 38 percent of the communication is through the tone of our voice, and the remaining 55 percent of how we communicate as humans is made up through our body language. Be intentional with your nonverbal communication as well as with your words.

Right Speech in Business

One of the fundamental rules of communication for leaders today is to praise in public and discipline in private. Our job is to inspire those we lead, not just incentivize them. Nobody wants to work for a leader who berates them in public. The people we lead want consistent feedback to help them learn and grow, so engage in walk-and-talks with your key reports, quarterly town halls where you share the state of the company or the department, aligning everyone's vision and recalibrating based on the last 90 days, and consistent reviews so they know what areas need to be improved, what they need to continue doing well, and you allow them an opportunity to share with you any insights that might not have been on your radar.

Be aware of your tone, vocabulary, and body language when you are speaking in a business setting. How we say something and our body language while we're saying it is the majority of how we communicate. Be mindful of your posture. Are your arms crossed? Do you look disengaged or uninterested while the other person is speaking? Or are you leaning forward, making eye contact, or maybe even mirroring their movements to show how laser-focused you are on their every word?

Poker players have mastered the art of nonverbal communication and picking up on even the subtest clues that can provide any information about their opponents. Something as inconsequential as a player looking at their chips after seeing their hand for the first time conveys tremendous information to an astute opponent. Subconsciously, when a poker player sees a strong hand, they immediately start to calculate the opportunity, which leads them to look at their chip stack for a fraction of a second. That's one thing poker players watch when opponents first look at their cards. If you watch any pro, they don't actually look at their cards until every person before them has acted. The most subtle change in body language tells a story to a trained observer. Was this person slumped back in their chair but then they subtly started leaning forward after looking at their cards? Or was there a change in the speed and way they placed the chips when calling or raising? How powerful is it in a business negotiation if you can read 90 percent of what the other person is feeling or thinking without them having to speak a word?

Cultivating Right Speech in the Workplace

Create a safe environment that encourages open communication and healthy debate. It's healthy and essential to ensure every voice in the room is heard. If their voice doesn't matter, there's a structural problem, and they shouldn't even be in the meeting or discussion. If their voice is valuable to the debate, it's your job as a leader to make sure they have a safe space to share ideas and concerns. There are no bad ideas in a brainstorming session. Nothing would infuriate me more than when, during a project ideation, someone in the meeting would shut down another team member while they were coming up with an idea to solve a problem. Even if that isn't the right solution, it could inspire a new thought in another team members that could be the cure for cancer.

Having that safe environment could also mean avoiding catastrophic consequences. Experts attribute the space shuttle Challenger disaster to groupthink failure. The decision to launch would have been avoided if everyone in the room felt comfortable sharing their concerns, but because of a desire to align with leadership goals at NASA, the decision to launch was made despite warnings about the potential problems with the O-rings. By worrying about not rocking the boat, they neglected to voice critical safety concerns, ultimately leading to one of the worst tragedies in NASA's history.

Tool: A Letter That Will Change a Life

If we're lucky, we've had multiple people who have touched us in such a unique way that it changes the trajectory of our lives. It could be a grandparent, a coach, or a mentor we meet on our path. The sad thing about touching someone's life in that way is that they may not know the impact for decades, and most will never find out. Think about the three people who had the most significant effect on becoming the person you are today. Write their names and how they touched your life. What was going on in your life, and what did they say or do that left such a significant mark that you are thinking about them right now? How did it change who you are today?

Mentor #1

_____

_____

(continued)

(*continued*)

_____

_____

_____

_____

_____

_____

_____

_____

_____

_____

Mentor #2

_____

_____

_____

_____

_____

_____

_____

_____

_____

_____

_____

Mentor #3

_____

_____

_____

_____

_____

_____

_____

_____

_____

_____

_____

_____

Are any of these people alive today? Whether it was your grandmother or your high school basketball coach, if you called them or wrote a letter sharing how they impacted your life in the same format here (what was going on in your life/how they touched you/the result it had), it would make their year. Don't waste opportunities like this. Maybe that person needs to hear from you today. We never know what someone else is going through at any given moment.

11

Zen and the Art of Communication

Communication is the most frequently reported challenge in organizations, from small companies to Fortune 500 enterprises. Applying effective communication techniques can transform culture, innovation, and profitability within any organization. Buddhists practice mindful listening, which is a part of Right Speech (see Chapter 10). Mindful listening means concentrating deeply and with compassion. Nhat Hanh said, "Compassionate listening helps the other side suffer less. If we realize that other people are the same people as we are, we are no longer angry at them."

As an organization scales, any breakdowns or challenges in communication will grow with the head count. Long gone are the days of interdepartmental envelopes and offices filled with three-ring binders of data. Today, mountains of data and the ability to create with a few keystrokes fit on a tool the size of a notebook along with literally thousands of ways to communicate. We get so many notifications on a daily basis across a multitude of channels that it becomes more complicated to communicate effectively. These tools also remove human face-to-face interaction from the workplace. Those in-person interactions do have substantial positive benefits and outcomes. I get more work done when I can be focused and without distraction, *and* I know the benefits of spending time in the room with people who are working toward the same objective. Even the organizations that are entirely remote invest in yearly, if not quarterly, company gatherings where the team can connect and collaborate. Connection is a big part of effective communication.

Challenges in Business Communication

Organizations large and small tend to have the same challenges with communication that typically fall into one or more of these six buckets: a **lack of clarity**, an **unsafe environment**, a **lack of transparency**, **disengagement**, confusion on **communication channels**, and the final and worst hurdle: **intentional misrepresentation**.

A Lack of Clarity

Lack of clarity usually falls into two categories. The first is a lack of clarity from the leadership to the masses about where the organization is going and what the plan is to get there. The second is poor one-on-one communications, either from manager to direct report or between peers. The good news is that lack of clarity is actually the most straightforward communication challenge to overcome.

Let's start with lack of clarity from leadership to the organization as a whole. Every company, no matter the size, must have a clear vision and values that are embraced and embodied by all. This should be communicated frequently and ideally displayed throughout an organization. Our core values and company vision were communicated at quarterly town halls where the leadership team gave examples of team members that embodied our values and shared transparently our progress toward the quarterly/yearly goals. Everyone in the company knew if we were on track or flailing based on the numbers we shared to start each quarter. We also reinforced our core values by giving out an award for each value to an employee who had displayed it over the previous quarter. While they were being recognized, the manager presenting the award would share the example of how the team member had displayed that core value. By consistently sharing where we planned to go along with the progress, including wins, setbacks, opportunities, and challenges, we stayed aligned as an organization. If times were challenging, it was better to communicate it to the people who could have the most impact on helping the organization overcome it. Remember, the best leaders give their teams credit for success and take responsibility when the team misses its goals.

One-to-one communication starts with a clear chain of command within the organization. Everyone within the company should have visibility into the organizational hierarchy, including responsibilities for each role. The first step is knowing who the right person is to be communicating with. Communication breaks down fundamentally when individuals bypass the chain of command.

When it comes to one-on-one communication, my good friend Ron Lovett uses a structure that consistently delivers clarity while being mindful of everyone involved. He divides it into three steps: **intention**, **outcome**, and **experience**.

- What is your **intention** in this meeting? It should lift the other person rather than only benefiting the company you represent or your personal agenda. View every interaction as an opportunity to create a win-win for all parties involved. When we are ethical in business dealings, making healthy profits is still very plausible.

- What is the desired **outcome**? This means you have a clearly defined vision for this meeting's result.

- Finally, how do you want the other people involved to **experience** you? What energy do you bring into the room? How does your body language tell a story?

Understanding your audience informs how you communicate clearly, utilizing these three steps. Be concise in your correspondence and avoid industry jargon or acronyms that might confuse the listener.

If you have anyone who reports directly, make sure they receive frequent feedback on their performance. Quarterly check-ins that measure how each team member is tracking their key performance indicators (KPIs) and any short or long-term goals are paramount for both the employee and the organization.

Another significant challenge we face today is that so much of our communication happens via email and text. With over 90 percent of a message conveyed through tone of voice and body language, we receive less than 10 percent of the original context when it's delivered electronically. Sentiment is easily misinterpreted, often leading to conflict and confusion. When we get confused or frustrated by a text, we need to start by always assuming positive intent. It's better to avoid assumptions that can lead to misunderstandings and ask for clarification and feedback. Once there's any misalignment that started from a text or email, rather than exacerbate the situation by responding using less than 10 percent of your communication ability, reply by asking to get on a call or, even better, a face-to-face meeting or video conference so you can clarify the sentiment and the message.

An Unsafe Environment

An **unsafe environment** that doesn't encourage everyone to have a voice stifles innovation while increasing the chance of failure. This type of workplace creates problems that could have been avoided if everyone felt comfortable speaking up. Groupthink can result in your best ideas never being brought to the table.

Worse than an atmosphere that doesn't foster collaboration and healthy debate is a toxic environment. No one should ever have to tolerate an unsafe workplace or personal space. Before you speak, let your words pass through three gates: Is it true? Is it necessary? Is it kind?

Most of the groundbreaking business ideas didn't come from a vacuum. The world's most successful businesses are never built on the back or brain of a single individual. When an organization doesn't foster a collaborative environment or, even worse, tolerates an unsafe environment, it's missing out on the most innovative ideas.

A Lack of Transparency

Transparency can be the difference between achieving our goals and failing when the result clearly should have been a successful outcome. I do not like keeping my team or friends in the dark. The one thing I learned over the years was that the more honest and vulnerable I was, the more people came to my aid in times of need. In the early days of running my agency, if somebody asked how things were going, even if I was on the verge of a nervous breakdown due to a cash flow crunch or missed client deadlines, my response was, "Things are great!" And I would continue to suffer alone. It wasn't until years later, after I joined EO (Entrepreneurs' Organization), that I realized being authentic and vulnerable about the challenges that we are facing is a superpower, not a weakness.

Being transparent does not mean being reckless. Know who you can trust and understand the importance of discretion and confidentiality. Common sense still prevails, and we want to make sure we're safe with intellectual property, confidential discussions regarding other people's business or personal lives, and, of course, your identity.

Disengagement

"Fools talk, cowards are silent, wise men listen." Listening is a required element in the alchemy of communicating. When the audience is **disengaged,** the message will be lost. Effective communication at even the most basic level requires a captive audience to receive the message and engage in the discussion.

There are a few tricks for dealing with a disengaged audience. The most important thing is removing the distraction of technology. I will not sit at a meal or have a coffee with another person who chooses to be on their phone. When I meet someone for coffee and we sit down and start conversing, if they look at their phone to respond to a message, I'll give them one pass. If they get on the phone the second time, I'll excuse myself and leave, letting them know that when they have time to be present, we can reschedule. Every minute of every day is a precious gift. Nobody should waste their time waiting while their companion responds to an email on their phone while sitting face to face. We live during an epidemic of distraction and disengagement. Take full advantage of the time we have with each other.

Confusion on Communication Channels

So much of our communication is lost in the multitude of platforms, channels, and applications we use within an organization. Having clearly defined **communication channels** that everyone understands and adheres to can remove confusion while keeping things from falling through the cracks. Define and stick to parameters around what type of communication is done on which channel. At my company, anything that required action was communicated via email. For real-time responses, we utilized Slack with different channels for the various departments, clients, general discussion, and where the team was going for lunch that day. It doesn't matter what your system is as long as it's understood and followed by everyone.

Intentional Misrepresentation

The final obstacle in communication is **intentional misrepresentation,** otherwise known as lying. It's impossible to be successful with dishonestly. When a part of the team is not being honest, it creates a toxic environment.

By utilizing tools like a company scorecard where each team member has a few KPIs they are accountable for and tracking velocity using a project management tool, it's possible to have accountability through transparency. Pro tip: If a member of the team doesn't want to use a customer relationship management (CRM) or project management tool, it's not because they don't need the tool. It's because they fear using it will pull the curtain back on their underperformance. In my experience, most of the team members who created an impression of being constantly working on overload were the lowest performers. Movement does not always equate to momentum. It's possible to look and act busy while accomplishing very little.

> *Speak only endearing speech, speech that is welcome. Speech, when it brings no evil to others, is a pleasant thing.*
>
> *—Buddha*

Tool: Business Communication Tools Defined

What tools does your organization use to communicate and stay connected as a cohesive team? Define how you communicate digitally, one on one, in teams, and as an entire organization.

Communications Channels

What tools does your organization use to communicate (email, WhatsApp, Slack, etc.)? Define the proper use of each tool, what type of communication it should be utilized for, and the expected response time for that channel.

_____

_____

_____

_____

_____

_____

_____

_____

_____

One-on-One Meetings

How frequently do team members meet one-on-one? What is the frequency of informal connections and the cadence/ format for goal setting, performance reviews, and feedback?

_____

_____

_____

_____

_____

_____

_____

_____

_____

_____

Team Meetings

What are the different meetings that need to happen within the organization? How can information be tracked and rolled up to the leadership team as leading indicators of success or failure? What is the agenda and cadence of the meetings? Who is in each meeting?

_____

_____

_____

_____

_____

_____

_____

_____

_____

Company Town Hall

What is the mechanism for communicating to the entire organization? What is the format and frequency of the company comprehensive meeting?

(continued)

(continued)

_____

_____

_____

_____

_____

_____

_____

_____

_____

_____

12

Right Action

Right Understanding, Right Thought, and Right Speech are the ways to prevent anything from arising that has the seed of ill will or bad intention. **Right Action** refers to avoiding causing harm to others, ourselves, and the planet. At the most fundamental level, this means living our lives with compassion and wisdom. Of course, this covers the basics of morality: do not steal, and do not kill or harm another. However, it goes deeper than simple instructions. Right Action is a moral compass that can be applied to every situation in all aspects of life.

If you light a lamp for someone else, it will also brighten your path.
—Buddha

Time: The Most Precious Resource

Right Action means prioritizing what matters most to us, focusing on relationships and family, and living our lives to the fullest potential. You might find it a little odd that in a book about the Zen of business, the first and most crucial action is family, which means you need to read this next part.

Do you know how a young child spells love? To them, love is not spelled L-O-V-E. They spell it T-I-M-E. Realize that how we spend our time speaks volumes about what we prioritize in our lives. Our time is the most precious resource we have and the only finite thing that you can never check the balance to see how much is remaining. Spend your time on the things that truly matter in life, and when the balance of your time runs out, you will have no regrets.

There is a fable about a mystical fox who had the power to see how long the animals in his forest would live. The animals formed a line and waited eagerly to learn their predetermined fates. First in line was Rabbit, who asked, "Fox, how long will I live?" Fox replied, "Rabbit, you will live for five years." Rabbit hopped away, happy in the knowledge that he had years to look forward to. The second in line was Tortoise; she asked, "Fox, how long will I live?" Fox replied, "Tortoise, you will live for over a century." Tortoise smiled as she slowly took her leave of Fox. Third in line was Monarch Butterfly, who had only emerged from his cocoon that morning, and he asked the same question: "Fox, how long will I live? Will it be a 100 years like Tortoise?" Fox looked at the Monarch Butterfly and replied, "I am sorry, Butterfly, but you will live for only two brief weeks."

Butterfly was devastated. He turned and flew away toward the field of grass and weeds where he was born, where he saw the most breathtaking female butterfly. "She's entirely out of my league," he thought, "but I'll be dead before I know it. So if today is one of my last days to live, what do I have to lose?" Emboldened by his newfound inspiration to seize the day, he flew over and introduced himself to the stunningly beautiful female butterfly. She was immediately captivated by him, and it was love at first sight. Together they flew along the field next to a small stream that eventually grew to become a vast river. The butterflies paused when they saw the river disappear over a cliff into a raging waterfall. A dragonfly joined them midflight as they contemplated whether to return or continue over the cliff. "Beware," said the dragonfly, "no one that follows the river ever returns!" Butterfly declared, "What do I have to lose? Life is brief and meant for living to the fullest," so they followed the waterfall over the cliff. The droplets drifting off the falling water created an awe-inspiring rainbow against the sky as they floated effortlessly down to the waterfall's base.

To their shock, when they had descended to the valley below, they found abundant fields of limitless wildflower varieties containing the most succulent nectars. For the rest of the day, the two butterflies basked in the sun, wildly in love and enjoying all of the gifts the world had to offer. As the sun set, they flew back up the cliff and followed the river back to Fox's den. Butterfly wanted to thank Fox for giving him the gift of knowing how little time he had so that he could have the courage to talk to the most beautiful potential mate and the perspective to push through his fears only to discover his nirvana. But Fox spoke first, "I am so sorry, Monarch Butterfly. I was wrong. Most live only two weeks, but you are the last generation of the season. You will live for nine more months."

Butterfly smiled and then took his turn to thank Fox for making the mistake. "Thinking I would be gone before seeing my first full moon," the butterfly said, "I have spent today like it would be my last. I spoke to the most beautiful girl that I would have never had the courage to before, and now we are in love. Together we ventured to a wondrous part of the forest over the waterfall to the endless field of wildflowers that the dragonfly said was too dangerous. I wouldn't have done these things if I thought I had more time. I wouldn't have taken the chance."

Fox laughed and asked, "How will you spend tomorrow now that you know you have so much life left to live?" To which the butterfly replied, "As if it were my last day alive."

Imagine what you would do with today if you knew it was the last day of your life. Now, live every day with that same intention and zest for life.

Act with Purpose

Right Action means taking action with intention. Things may come to those who wait, but only what is left by those who hustle. Your actions should harm no one nor create suffering for yourself along the way, but make no mistake, achieving anything worthwhile requires effort. It means being intentional with your capacity each day. Each of us has the same 24 hours a day, but a few people seem to routinely complete tasks that build into significant accomplishments, while others give the impression of being overwhelmed while making little or no progress. The key to finishing anything isn't bursts of intense effort; it's actually simply consistently showing up. (See Figure 12.1.)

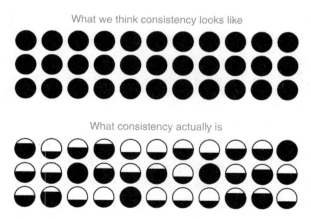

FIGURE 12.1 What consistency looks like.
Source: Keith Roberts.

Focus on your daily actions over the next year, and you will be astonished by the transformation that will take place. After 365 days of methodically embracing the habits and behaviors that help you grow personally and professionally, you will be a different person. Remember that consistency does not mean hitting it out of the park every single day of the week. Consistency is also those days when you hardly have it in you and you still make incremental progress. It's the days when you fall short and keep going the next day without giving up.

One trick I use is the two times rule. If there is a healthy practice I am trying to create or a habit that doesn't serve me that I am trying to free myself from, I never do it for more than two consecutive days if I fall off my routine. For example, if your goal is daily meditation and you miss a day on a busy day of travel, make sure not to miss the practice tomorrow. Never going two consecutive days makes it possible to allow imperfection, but it's methodical enough to ensure you stay on track.

Right Action in Business

Right Action also means putting 100 percent effort into anything you say yes to. Thomas Edison said, "Opportunity is missed by most people because it is dressed in overalls and looks like work." There couldn't be a more accurate statement. Think about it: If knowledge equaled results, most people would have six-pack abs. We all know what is required to be in good physical shape—it takes exercise and a healthy diet. Yet we live in a time with the worst epidemic of obesity in human history. We know what it takes to accomplish our goals, but 99 percent of the world's population won't come close to reaching their full potential.

It's not enough to have the right mindset to manifest the desired outcome; we have to make continuous progress toward our goal. We must push forward every day, even on those days when we face the most significant opposition and don't know where we will find the willpower. I believe in the power of an abundance mindset versus scarcity thinking when it comes to attracting opportunities, but that's not enough. When an opportunity presents itself, we need to spring into action and do the work required to be successful.

Be not afraid of going slowly, be afraid only of standing still.
—*Eastern Proverb*

Our habits shape our future. The small things done every day add up to the quality of our lives we will experience. This is where consistency comes in again. Making consistent progress toward our goals will always outperform short bursts of excitement with extreme effort. Slow and steady does win the race. That pace also allows for balance. When we burn the candle at both ends for business, it takes a toll on our relationships in addition to negatively affecting our physical and mental well-being.

Your actions in business matter because you set the example for what's acceptable within the organization you lead. The saying "Do as I say, not as I do" does not work. Our employees and our children will mirror your behavior. Lead by example by following through on your commitments and consistently delivering on time. I can't tell you how many times in my professional career, a vendor promised a proposal by a particular day, and a week later, I would still be waiting to receive it. If you can't keep your commitment to sending over the proposal, it's impossible to trust you to deliver the product or service you're trying to sell me on time.

A close friend, Kym Huynh, always says, "Let's just do it now." When something presents itself to be done, that is Kym's mantra: "Let's just do it now." I love this approach and embrace a technique called the **Two-Minute Rule**. Anything that comes across my to-do list, if it takes less than two minutes, I will do it immediately. Studies have shown that it takes more time to come back and reread the email or listen to the voicemail before responding rather than "Let's just do it now."

The best example of how essential **Daily Progress** is in reaching our objectives was the two expeditions to the South Pole. In 1911, two expeditions set out to be the first explorers to reach the South Pole. The first expedition was led by Robert Falcon Scott, and the second expedition was led by a Norwegian explorer, Roald Amundsen. For these expeditions, the difference between success and failure was that one group made progress every day, no matter how horrific the conditions were, and the other let circumstances (the weather) dictate progress. Rather than stick to the plan and continue to make progress when things got tough, they would hunker down during the storms and wait for ideal circumstances to make up for lost time.

Amundsen's expedition marched 20 miles a day, regardless of how challenging the circumstances were. The Amundsen team reached the South Pole 35 days before Scott's expedition, and when the British finally arrived, they found a green tent left by Amundsen's group that had arrived exactly on schedule, the very day they had planned to reach the South Pole. Not only did the British team get beaten to the South Pole, but those men tragically lost their lives on the return trek. For those men, the stakes of daily progress were a matter of life and death. For each of us, the stakes are actually the same. Today is a gift, and tomorrow is not guaranteed. What are you doing today to make progress toward reaching your goals?

Successful people are not gifted; they just work hard, then succeed on purpose.

—*G.K. Nielson*

Tool: Aligning Our Priorities and Our Actions

At any given time in our lives, our priorities can change. This is different from our core values, which are ingrained in us at a young age. Depending on the chapter of life we're currently in, our priorities could shift from adventure to fatherhood to legacy and beyond. What matters is how we spend our time right now. Are we aligning our most precious resource, time, with what we say are the five priorities in our lives?

What are your five priorities in life right now?

1. _____
   _____
   _____
   _____

2. _____
   _____
   _____
   _____

3. _____
   _____
   _____
   _____

4. _____
   _____
   _____
   _____

5. _____

_____

_____

_____

Color-code your calendar to see how much of it is spent on each of these priorities. With time as our most precious resource, make sure to align it with your priorities. If family is one of the top five that make this list, but you spend a fraction of your time with them, your actions don't align with your priorities, Actions speak louder than words. Align what matters with how you spend that one finite resource: your time.

CHAPTER

13

Embracing Your Inner Monk

Right Action is embracing your inner monk and executing on the vision for reaching your full potential. Right Understanding and Right Thought are limited without taking Action. This means treating our bodies like the temples they are and embracing mindfulness for our mental well-being.

The word *Zen* simply means meditation. The practice of Zen is mindful meditation and actions so that we live compassionate and healthy lives. It's tragically become a badge of honor in our society to be a workaholic. People talk about the crazy hours as if that does not have a negative impact on their relationships and personal lives while they damage their physical and mental health by burning the candle at both ends. So much of the stress we feel is self-imposed. The negative habits we've created, like waking up and immediately reading emails on our phones when we haven't even gotten out of bed, are unhealthy. The reality is unless you're an obstetrician or a neurosurgeon, you don't need to look at your phone for at least 30 minutes after you wake up in the morning.

Starting the Day Off Right

I advocate starting each day with one of two different practices, either the **10-10-10 Morning Routine** or the **Flow State Routine**. Both of these practices set you up for creative thinking, problem-solving, and maximizing productivity. Both the 10-10-10 Morning and Flow State Routines techniques deliver consistent results for the practitioner. Choose a system that works for your performance and happiness.

The 10-10-10 Morning Routine

My personal favorite way to start each day is Warren Rustand's **10-10-10 Morning Routine**, which is 10 minutes of meditation, followed by 10 minutes of reading, and ending with 10 minutes of journaling. The advantages of starting each morning with this 30-minute routine are transformational:

- Meditation is proven to reduce stress, boost creativity, increase attention span, and even decrease blood pressure. (Find out more about meditation later in this chapter.)
- Reading helps retain information and improves memory and cognitive abilities.
- Journaling aligns our intentions, unblocks the ego, and doubles the probability of anything you write down.

Taking half an hour each morning before diving into your day primes you for success. This process of starting each day will result in increased productivity, innovation, and creativity at work while simultaneously reducing stress and boosting happiness.

The Flow State Routine

Some prefer the **Flow State Routine** for its exponentially increased output. The Flow State Routine consists of three components: planning, focused work, and active recovery.

- **Planning** prior to the first sprint aligns with what needs to be done. This should be done the day before so that as soon as you wake up in the morning, you start the first two-hour block of focused work.

- During the **focused work**, turn off all distractions. Close your email application, put your phone on silent mode, and focus on the list of tasks with your undivided attention. When we can get into the flow state of focus, our brain is between the alpha and theta brain waves. This state amplifies our ability to solve complex problems and innovate. Everything else fades away as we zero in on our task at hand. What can be accomplished in a short amount of time with that level of focus is mind-blowing and also exhausting. Before stopping your session, create and prioritize the tasks list for the second two-hour focused work block, then step away.

- Once the two-hour sprint is completed, you will need to recover. **Active recovery** is shown to help our mind and body bounce back faster than passive recovery. Mediation, yoga, or your activity of choice is better than taking a break and watching TV. Have some kind of nutrition to refuel, then turn off email and devices again to begin the second two hours of focused work block.

For your next block, start with the most critical item on the list and work on that until it is complete, then move on to the next item until your two hours are done. After the block of focus, work closely with another active recovery and plan tomorrow's priority task.

Why We Meditate

Meditation is the most common practice among the world's happiest and highest-performing humans. Tragically, many people abandon the practice before seeing the benefits, usually because they struggle to get started. One of the biggest challenges with contemplative, concentrated, or even guided meditations is that thoughts enter our minds while we are meditating. Many people feel they don't understand how to meditate and immediately abandon it. The reality is that even the most seasoned veteran meditators, at times, have thoughts that enter their minds. The brief moments that we have in meditation when our mind is totally at peace with itself are euphoric and where some of our most innovative and creative ideas come from. Michael Jordan said, "If a child is learning to walk and falls down 50 times, they never think to themselves, 'This isn't for me.'" Meditation is as consequential to the human race as learning to walk.

Some people hesitate to embrace meditation because of their spiritual or religious views. I promise you that meditation will not turn you into a long-haired Buddhist like me. What will happen is a decisive shift in your mental state for the better. People from all over the world, spanning all possible spiritual and religious beliefs, practice meditation. It is not worshiping a false deity or taking away from your personal religious practice. Think about it this way: When you are praying, you are speaking to your God, and when you practice meditation, you are listening to God.

Being a Warrior Monk in Business

Become a warrior monk in life and business. Shaolin monks are known for their physical strength, mental stamina, and unparalleled discipline. Their inner strength comes from the belief that they can overcome any obstacle. The first teaching of the

Shaolin philosophy is that discipline leads to self-control. Without discipline, reaching our true potential is unattainable. The Shaolin monks are known for accomplishing seemingly impossible physical and mental feats. Become a warrior monk.

Patience and Discipline

A vital principle in the Shaolin monks' practice is **practice patience**. When we are trying to build something new in business, remember that it takes time to do hard things. Look at it from the perspective of being grateful that it's hard to accomplish your goals. If it were easy, everyone would do it.

Discipline is the difference between dreaming about our objectives and accomplishing them. There is a Zen proverb: "Before enlightenment, chop wood, carry water. After enlightenment, chop wood, carry water." This is one of my most revered Buddhist teachings. A student asked, "How do I reach enlightenment?" and the answer was, "Do your work." At the time that this was spoken, water and wood would have been essential to sustain life. These two tasks are some of the most tedious and must be done daily. They were arguably the two most important tasks for survival when the student asked Buddha how he could get past the suffering of daily life. "What do we do when we are enlightened?" To which the Buddha replies, "Chop wood, carry water." The answer is that despite the fact that nothing seems to have changed from the outside, everything actually has changed inside, with our awareness and understanding.

Self-Care

Self-care should not be confused with "self-cherishing," which is our mind thinking, "I am special and vital while neglecting others." One of the things that we must do for ourselves and to be better for our employees and families is self-care. Sadly, it's become a badge of honor to be a workaholic and neglect what's really important in life in exchange for the pursuit that feeds our ego and material desires. Not only do you deserve and have every right to take exceptional care of yourself, but it's actually your responsibility.

When I was struggling in a particularly dark time both professionally and in my personal life, a good friend of mine, Susan, looked at me and said, "You have to put on your own oxygen mask first." At that moment, it hit me like a ton of bricks. I had a habit of putting off self-care and essential tasks that would benefit my business to help others when, in reality, the most important thing I needed to do at those times was take care of my own house.

There is a reason the flight attendants review the safety instructions on a flight every single time. If you fail to make sure you stay conscious during the flight emergency, it's impossible to help anyone else. It's the same in life. If we don't care for ourselves, we won't be around to care for the ones we care about.

Getting enough sleep is one of the most important things you can do and the greatest gift you can give your body and mind. We live surrounded by distractions, and our attention spans have decreased to nanoseconds. Sleep is when our body is healing itself. It's essential to get at least seven or eight hours of sleep every night. If you struggle to get to sleep, try turning off your devices an hour before you go to bed. Practice meditation, read a book, or do something other than look at pixels to let your mind unwind from the day.

Avoid using pharmaceuticals to aid in sleep. If you struggle to fall asleep, try box breathing. Box breathing is a technique where you inhale and count 1-2-3-4, then hold your breath and count 1-2-3-4, exhale and count 1-2-3-4, and hold again for 1-2-3-4. Make a box in your mind as you're counting, and after several cycles, extend it to a count of 1-2-3-4-5. This technique calms your nervous system, reduces heart rate, decreases stress, and helps regulate your mood by distracting us from anything other than counting and breathing. It's an exceptional technique to help you fall asleep before trying pharmaceutical options that can be addictive and have side effects.

When you wake up in the morning, instead of immediately drinking a pot of coffee and diving into your email, drink a glass of warm lemon water with a tablespoon of pink Himalayan sea salt. This will finish flushing out the toxins that your body was dealing with while you slept and will hydrate you to start your day.

Take the time when you first wake up to prime your body for the day. Stretch, get out in the sun, move your body, and find the morning routine that works best for you, whether it's embracing Warren's **10-10-10**, possibly the **Flow State Routine,** or whatever version of a healthy morning works to optimize your mind and body. Don't feel you need to replicate what you see hustle-preneurs doing on social media. Do what works for you, be disciplined, and be a Warrior Monk.

Tool: Creating Your Routines

Focus on your daily actions over the next year. Three hundred sixty-five days of conditioning our habits and behaviors with how we start and end each day will transform our lives. Remember not to look at screens for at least 30 minutes after waking up in the morning or 30 minutes before going to sleep. Include the time it takes you to do each part of your routine and plan for it.

Morning routine:

_____

_____

(continued)

(*continued*)

_____

_____

_____

_____

_____

_____

_____

Evening routine:

_____

_____

_____

_____

_____

_____

_____

_____

_____

CHAPTER

14

Forest Bathing (Shinrin Yoku)

Spending time in nature is the fundamental practice that aligns Right Action with our practice of self-care. Shinrin Yoku is the Japanese practice of "forest bathing." This doesn't mean hugging a tree; it is simply spending time in nature. Leave your phone behind and just wander through a park. There is no need to run or climb a mountain (although these activities will never take away from the benefits); you can even sit if you want and just appreciate the sights, sounds, and smells of being in nature. The clean, fragrant air and fractal patterns in trees and bushes help us reduce cortisol and increase serotonin and oxytocin, and it takes only 20 minutes in nature to start having meaningful results that can be measured scientifically.

Studies have shown that practicing Shinrin Yoku helps with focus, decreases stress levels, helps with sleep, and reduces depression. Studies have shown that forest bathing has led to a healthier lifestyle for people of all ages in their population. It makes sense when you think about it. Our brains have not evolved as quickly as cities have. Only a few hundred years ago, wild animals could potentially and routinely end our lives by having us for dinner. When the bushes rustled in the forest, our ancestors' bodies flooded with adrenaline, their pupils dilated, and they could run further and faster to stay alive. Unfortunately, our neurochemistry has not evolved as fast as the safety of the modern world.

That means we're getting the same neurotransmitters releasing cortisol when we are late for an important work meeting that our ancestors received when it was truly a matter of life and death. To exacerbate this problem, we have removed ourselves from nature and migrated into cities filled with people, noise pollution, Wi-Fi, and an endless amount of stimulation, preventing our minds from resetting back to a relaxed state. The fractal patterns that appear in nature reduce the cortisol (stress hormone). Now that you understand your mind is already overreacting to things that are not as significant as living or dying, something must be done to create balance from the chaos.

In a world of quick fixes and pills to solve our problems, who would have thought the remedy for what seems like such an insurmountable obstacle to overcome is simply getting out into nature? Forest bathing as a practice dates back to the 1980s in Japan. At that time the world was becoming aware of the impact that unhealthy lifestyles had on our minds and bodies. The same cities that provide safety, convenience, and connection are having a negative effect on our mental well-being and physical health.

Practicing Shinrin Yoku (Even at Work)

The standard practice of Shinrin Yoku is spending 20 minutes three times a week in nature. This can be as simple as going for a walk in your local park with your dog or taking a hike on the closest trail. The compelling truth about forest bathing is how profoundly simple it is. There are no gym memberships required or equipment to be purchased before you can start this life-changing practice. All you need is a pair of walking shoes and a bottle of water to start.

This practice is so essential, I advocate that everyone schedule this time on their calendar every week to guarantee it happens. There genuinely is no excuse for missing a 20-minute walk in a park. It doesn't matter if you're on the road or in the busiest city in the world; there is always a patch of nature to take a stroll.

One of my favorite hacks is having a walk-and-talk instead of a Zoom meeting or conference call. It's scientifically proven that if we're walking, we're being more creative. It's also a way to move our bodies instead of being stuck at a desk staring at a screen. Take just one of your meetings every day while walking in a park and start enjoying the benefits of Shinrin Yoku.

In addition to the weekly practice, I take a two-hour forest bath once a month. It's like a jump-start that will bring you into the present while helping eliminate the stresses of living in a modern city. I love to couple this with a long hike that includes at least one meditation along the way. Some of you reading this right now think there's no way you could take two hours a month to walk in the woods. What if you knew that some of the most profound innovations that changed the course of human history and some of the art that we hold so dear to our hearts were inspired by brief walks in nature? Neil Young wrote the song "Ohio" after seeing the tragic images of the Kent State shootings; he famously disappeared into the woods and emerged a short time later with one of the most potent and profound songs of all time.

Just Go Camping

The yearly Shinrin Yoku practice is 72 hours in nature without technology. This is a mere three days, a long weekend away from the city and your phone. Still, many resist this opportunity to reset their minds while having real experiences. Three days a year with no technology is a digital detox that helps achieve better sleep, lowers blood pressure, and reduces anxiety—ailments for which we are constantly bombarded with pharmaceutical commercials to cure. The difference is that there are no adverse side effects, and the benefits are extraordinary.

First of all, there is a significant decrease in stress, depression, and anxiety than prior to going into the woods. Studies have also shown that being outdoors can benefit your heart health by lowering blood pressure and cholesterol and improving circulation and heart strength. Better sleep is always a result of time away from technology, and getting outside can actually add years to our lives. Spending time in nature supports an increased lifespan; several studies have linked time and nature to reducing the risk of chronic conditions like heart disease, obesity, and diabetes. The mental benefits have also been proven from better cognition, increased memory, and an increase in innovation and creativity when we return to our daily lives.

Time in nature should not be viewed as a luxury but as an important part of our health and well-being. Our connection to nature is an essential part of being alive. Getting into nature, even for short periods, improves our mood and creativity, reduces stress cortisol levels, and improves our cognitive performance. Science has shown that nature's fractal patterns and the sounds of birds help us feel calm and alert. Even the smell of pine trees can help strengthen our immune system. You were meant to be in nature, not a conference room. For many of us, it's a part of life that we spend hours a day looking at computer screens, commuting in congested traffic, or communicating with technology rather than human connection. It is so vital that in Nordic countries, access to nature is considered a human right.

I went to the woods because I wished to live deliberately, to front only the essential facts of life, and see if I could not learn what it had to teach, and not, when I came to die, discover that I had not lived. I did not wish to live what was not life, living is so dear; nor did I wish to practice resignation, unless it was quite necessary. I wanted to live deep and suck out all the marrow of life, to live so sturdily and Spartan-like as to put to rout all that was not life, to cut a broad swath and shave close, to drive life into a corner, and reduce it to its lowest terms.

—Henry David Thoreau

Tool: Forest Bathing

If you start practicing Shinrin Yoku, the benefits will be experienced immediately. Begin with the essential three times a week for 20 minutes. After practicing for a few weeks and realizing the impact it has had, schedule your two-hour monthly forest bath and make it a recurring habit. After a few months of experiencing the profound effect of only 2 hours, it's time to schedule the 72-hour nature experience. Plan someplace that you have wanted to visit that has an inspiring landscape.

Weekly Shinrin Yoku

What are three places close to your home where you can practice Shinrin Yoku? It can be a local park or a natural setting that is less than a 20-minute drive from your home or office.

_____

_____

(continued)

(continued)

Monthly Forest Bath

What are three places close to your home where you can practice Shinrin Yoku monthly?

_____

_____

_____

Yearly 72 Hours in Nature

Where will you travel for the three days in nature? What resources do you need? Will this be a solo trip or a group experiencing the same digital detox that has aligned goals for the time in nature? What activities will you do? Plan for the food and other logistics.

_____

_____

_____

_____

_____

_____

_____

_____

15

Right Livelihood

How do we earn the necessities in life? Right Livelihood is making a living through a means that does no harm to ourselves or others. Buddha believed that we could find a career that would be meaningful and rewarding while following the Middle Path. Think about how your work impacts those around you and the planet. It is possible to do work that is authentic and ethical in which the customer receives exceptional value for the product and service delivered, and the organization providing the product or service makes a fair profit. That profit should be equitably distributed throughout the organization. One of the world's biggest issues today is the ever-growing gap between the ultra-wealthy and the working class. We have a tremendous problem to resolve as a society when, at the same time as having the highest number of billionaires, we also face the worst epidemic of homelessness in modern times.

Right Livelihood illustrates the importance of contributing to the well-being of others, relieving suffering, cultivating wisdom, and bringing happiness into the world. Almost everyone is required to provide through a career that must be integrated into their spiritual practice and beliefs. Many of us spend the majority of our lives at our craft, so it's essential to understand how what we do for work affects our hearts and minds. It is possible to engage in meaningful work that does not hinder our spiritual growth but instead helps us evolve.

Avoiding Harm and Finding Balance

Are you causing harm in your profession? The bar at my agency, Zenman, was always "Would I show my mom?" We wouldn't take any clients or do any work at the agency that I wouldn't proudly show my mom. Remember, when I started my digital agency, the only thing that made money online was adult content— not something I wanted to show my mom. Back when I had the brilliant idea to start a website agency, Amazon was still losing money. To be exact, in 1998, the year I started Zenman, Amazon had a net loss of $124.5 million. Adult content websites generated almost a billion dollars in profit in the same year, and we received offers to work on these websites. Even when I desperately needed the revenue, the answer was always "No."

Buddha specified five types of businesses that we should not engage in: Dealings with Weapons, Trade of Humans (slavery and prostitution), Meat Butchery, Dealings with Intoxicants, and Dealings with Poison. When I compare the bar I set at the agency, "what I wouldn't show my mom" aligns perfectly. The five types of businesses that Buddha advocated for us not to engage in are the same ones that already didn't feel right for me morally. It does not exclude a significant amount of the opportunity that exists in the world today. Would you really want to work in an industry that you know causes harm?

Once we find a business that aligns with our zone of genius and doesn't harm ourselves or others, it's time to find the balance. Over the years, I've had the privilege of meeting several billionaires and speaking to them about their journeys. Frequently, their stories are shocking as they openly shared the tremendous sacrifices they make to their families and their physical health, which they take accountability for in pursuit of their financial goals. What is the cost of the success you're pursuing?

My friend Ron Lovett has the perfect perspective on this. When it comes to business, this guy loves hunting down new deals, negotiating the best possible terms, and creating wins for his partners and his customers. Ron owns VIDA, a housing company based in Halifax, Nova Scotia, Canada, which has raised the standard for attainable rental communities in Canada. Ron started VIDA after exiting his private security company, and at the same time he was starting a family. If you know Ron, you know the guy is ferocious. When he was doing private security, he traveled to Thailand to study bare-knuckle boxing with the best in the world, and he is the guy you want on your side in any situation. I am in awe of this man, and we haven't gotten to the really impressive aspect of Mr. Lovett.

As Ron has built VIDA, he had a goal of scaling the number of communities to have the most significant possible impact on the families he served. Unlike the other moguls of industry who sacrificed family for profit, Ron has always maintained his family-first mindset. Nothing comes before his wife and children. Right Livelihood also means that we understand how our work impacts our relationships and those we love the most.

Right Livelihood in Business

It seems redundant to discuss Right Livelihood in business; however, it is advantageous to ensure your personal core values and purpose in this life align with the business that you lead. When we are inspired professionally, it's easier to look forward to Monday mornings and new projects. When there is no line between what we do to earn a living and how we spend our free time, we have found our Ikigai (see more in Chapter 16).

In Daniel Pink's groundbreaking book *Drive: The Surprising Truth About What Motivates Us*, he challenges the traditional concept of financial incentives to motivate performance and illustrates how people are driven more by purpose, autonomy, and mastery. Pink found that a traditional reward-based model was much less motivating than engaging in something you believed was a worthy pursuit.

Using Business Success to Make the World a Better Place

Business success also empowers us to change the world. Jeff Hoffman was one of the most powerful keynote speakers I have had the privilege to see in person. He has had a series of significant business exits and won a Grammy and an Emmy, but the story that really moved me happened after his first exit. Jeff was the guy who came up with the self-check-in kiosks at airports. It happened out of necessity when he was running late for a flight when he was young, and he asked everyone in line waiting to check in at the counter if they would use an automated system. Of course, the long line of impatient travelers eagerly reinforced his initial research, and Jeff went on to create airline check-in kiosks and had a healthy exit while still a very young man.

After his exit, Jeff tells a story of sitting at home watching football one night when the game was interrupted by a breaking news story about a women's shelter that was being closed. The story was heartbreaking; the two women who had started the shelter had invested everything into it, and the next day they would be losing it to foreclosure. The residents who needed protection from abusive spouses or exes would be out on the street, and the children would have no place to call home. Jeff thought to himself, "Somebody should do something." Then he realized there was no "somebody" and that *he* needed to do something.

Jeff went to the bank the next day and withdrew such a large amount of cash that the teller initially thought he was trying to rob the bank. He took that money to the shelter the day the women thought they were losing it. He anonymously gave them enough cash to pay off the mortgage, installed a security system to ensure the residents were safe, and established a childcare program that empowered the women who lived in the shelter to rebuild their careers and stand on their own. Jeff did this anonymously because it was the right thing to do; now it's well known, along with dozens of other stories, that his humanitarian efforts have made the world a better place, one person at a time. Jeff Hoffman is an example of how you can use extraordinary business success to fuel the work that brings joy to our hearts and transforms the lives of others.

Right Livelihood goes beyond not doing harm; it means contributing to the greater good. It can be done without sacrificing our family and in harmony with what we need to take care of ourselves.

Tool: What Good Shall I Do this Day?

Benjamin Franklin would answer the question "What good shall I do this day?" every morning before he got out of bed. Set your intentions for the day as a part of your daily routine. Align your daily activities with your goals and priorities. Start with one year out from today and clearly state your intentions, and include how this makes you feel. Then break it down into where you need to

(*continued*)

(continued)

be in 90 days to reach that goal and clearly articulate those key performance indicators (KPIs). Finally, state your intention for today that aligns with the goals you want to achieve in the future.

Intention for one year from today (include feelings once you have accomplished):

_____

_____

_____

_____

_____

_____

Create a SMART (simple, measurable, attainable, relevant, and time-bound) goal that represents where you need to be in 90 days to be on track with reaching your one-year goal:

_____

_____

_____

_____

_____

_____

With **clarity of vision**, state your intention for the day:

_____

_____

_____

_____

_____

CHAPTER

16

Ikigai

Ikigai (*pronounced ee-kee-guy*, not *icky-guy*) is a Japanese concept that combines two words (*iki*, meaning "to live," and *gai*, meaning "reason") and translates to "Reason for Living." The concept empowers one to find their true life's purpose and then get on the path to living their best life. We have all heard Warren Beatty's saying, "You've achieved success in your field when you don't know whether what you're doing is work or play." That is the most basic explanation of Ikigai: You love what you do so much that it's no longer work, it's your purpose.

The Western interpretation of Ikigai focuses on our professional life, while the traditional Japanese concept could refer to a hobby, family, partner, or profession. The Western interpretation of Ikigai (see Figure 16.1) is distilled into a Venn diagram where your Ikigai sits at the center of these elements:

- What the world needs
- What we are good at

163

- What we love
- What we can be paid for

This framework is an excellent structure for finding the Right Livelihood (covered in Chapter 15), but it is not an accurate representation of the traditional concept of Ikigai. Ikigai is not the pursuit of professional recognition or material gain. Success may be a by-product of living your life purpose, but it should not be the focus. We must first and foremost focus on being present in the now and finding joy in our daily lives.

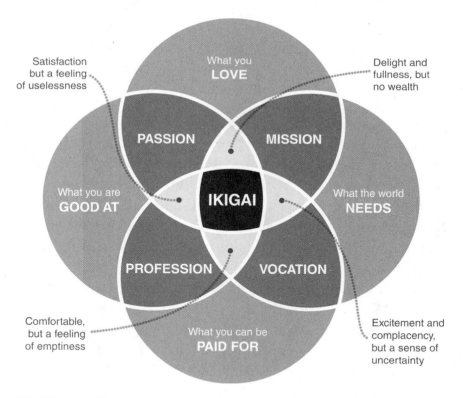

FIGURE 16.1 The Western interpretation of Ikigai.

Source: Keith Roberts.

The Magic of Ikigai

In the East, Ikigai creates a life worth living, but it is not always connected to our livelihood. Ikigai gives value to our lives, making them worthwhile. The feelings of living our Ikigai are:

- Purpose and fulfillment
- Motivation
- Self-control
- Gratitude
- Self-realization

Rather than ask yourself, "What do you love, can be paid for, that you are good at and the world needs?" ask, "What **motivates** you while creating a sense of **purpose and fulfillment?** What inspires you to have passionate **discipline** and genuine **gratitude** while working toward **self-realization?**"

Purpose and Fulfillment

Try to find purpose in something that fills you with joy—the thing that gets you out of bed every morning and motivates you to continue marching forward, even on the most challenging days. What fills your cup? What do you love so much that you would do it even if you weren't being paid? What is that rare gift that others see in you, something that appears challenging for most, but it brings you happiness? It should create a feeling of accomplishment that encourages you to follow this passion and embrace it with 100 percent of your effort.

Motivation

Your Ikigai is a motivating force that fuels you. It should be a perpetual energy source, not one that requires constant replenishment. Imagine your Ikigai is something that fills your cup rather than draining it while engaging in the activity or relationship. That doesn't mean we won't face adversity and challenging times; it means we are unconditionally motivated to continue even in the face of the most testing times. It is literally what drives you forward in the face of adversity. What is it that is so meaningful to you that it would inspire you to move mountains?

Self-Control

The difference between having a dream and making it a reality lies in our self-control and discipline. Anything is possible with the mindset of putting off what we want today for what we want tomorrow. There is nothing that can't be built or changed over time when we have the patience and discipline to work consistently toward our goal.

Gratitude

Gratitude constantly recalibrates our perspective on what's truly important in life. It's become one of the cornerstones of most methodologies today in personal growth, self-care, and beyond. Gratitude truly is a superpower, but the magic gets lost if we just walk through the motions. Make sure not to repeat things that you're grateful for when thinking about them, or you get diminishing returns on the practice.

To get the most ROI (return on investment) from your gratefulness practice, actually feel the gratitude instead of just writing it down or thinking about it. With your heart, feel gratitude for whatever you're grateful for. If you struggle with things to be thankful for every day that isn't repetitive, think about some of the struggles in the world you will never face. A billion people on Earth today don't have access to safe drinking water. I promise you there is somebody in a hospital bed right now who would chop off their left arm to trade problems with you.

Self-Realization

Merriam-Webster defines self-realization as "fulfillment by oneself of the possibilities of one's character or personality." It is accomplished through discovering and living our fullest potential in this life. This requires transcending the limitations of our ego, allowing us to experience a connection with the world and all living beings. Self-realization brings harmony, contentment, and inner peace, which are unattainable from material wealth, shedding light on the true meaning of life. Self-realization is the most advanced need in Abraham Maslow's Hierarchy of Needs (although he calls it self-actualization).

Finding My Ikigai

The quest to discover my Ikigai was a journey on which I left no stone unturned. It took trips to the jungles of South America and sacred plant medicine ceremonies, as well as years of meditation, several intensive weeklong workshops, personal therapy, a few pilgrimages, and a lot of deep contemplation. I can say with confidence now that **my purpose is to inspire a billion humans and provide them with the tools to reach nirvana**. My goal in this life is to be a Bodhisattva who helps others live their best possible lives and achieve enlightenment.

The journey to finding my Ikigai was prolonged by my inner struggle to try to frame my life's purpose around the company I had spent two decades building through my blood, sweat, and tears. My agency was literally called Zenman because, in the beginning, it was just me, a Buddhist dude, cranking out websites under the stairs in my living room. I continued to hold on to the sunk equity I had built in the business. After all, it had provided me with a comfortable life, at least from the outside, but I had lost all passion for agency life. To be completely honest, I don't think I ever had it. I was good at it, and it paid really well, but commercial art can be soul-sucking. My true love has always been photography.

The business had, however, become my identity. When people thought about Zenman, they associated it with me, and when I met someone new, the agency's reputation preceded my own. It didn't help that my nickname was literally the same as the company's nomenclature. I was "the Zenman."

For most of the years I ran the agency, there was a connection between my feeling of personal worth that was tied to the success and reputation of the agency. When the company struggled, I was depressed and struggled along with it. There was an unhealthy correlation between my business and my identity. Even though there were years when the agency and I personally made a lot of money, I was still trading my time for money. The only finite resource I had was being sold at an hourly rate. Granted, that rate was really, really high, but that didn't change the fact that it was still a bad deal. Something had to change within me. I made a conscious shift to move away from the business I had spent my entire adult life building toward an unknown future that I felt was my authentic calling. The result is the book you are holding in your hands.

What Is Your Why?

Living your Ikigai means cultivating your capacity, ensuring you live up to your true potential. Dan Sullivan wrote, "Someone once told me the definition of hell: The last day you have on

Earth, the person you became will meet the person you could have become." Imagine the disappointment that most people would experience if this were true. Spend the rest of your life with the assumptions that you will meet your true potential one day. If we miss out on essential lessons in this life, we will be forced to repeat them. Or worse, if we behave in a way that is harmful to our Karma, it is creating a more challenging future for ourselves.

Simon Sinek has taught us the importance of starting with the *why*—the purpose, cause, and belief of your organization. Exceptional organizations have a why that is easy to understand and shared by all. It's the secret sauce that sets organizations apart from the competition. What is your why? Have you found your personal purpose, cause, and passion? Life is not meant to be a drawn-out expression of someone else's expectations. Start on the path to finding your why today.

It's never too late to start. The odds that you even exist are mind-bogglingly low: 1 in 400,000,000,000. This life is a tremendous gift just to be alive. Embrace this opportunity to find your purpose. Whether you call it your why or Ikigai, follow your unique path and leave no stone unturned on your journey to finding your reason for living. Buddha said, "Your purpose in life is to find your purpose and give your whole heart and soul to it."

Happiness and Longevity

Okinawa has one of the longest life expectancies in the world; 68 out of every 100,000 people in Okinawa will live to be over a century old. This is three times the number of centenarians in the United States. Many factors contribute to this, including their diet of whole foods and the climate, but one critical factor is that they know and live their Ikigai.

In addition to having a purpose in life to inspire you to keep living a full and long life, the second contributing factor to longevity is having a community. Friends bring us joy and connection, and studies have shown the benefits of having a healthy social life contribute to an increased life expectancy. Having a social network (of real people, not online) has been demonstrated in multiple studies to increase our lifespan. There is something about having others that we care about and look forward to seeing that makes life worth living compared to our peers who don't have the same connection. Friends bring us joy and laughter, and it results in increased longevity.

Tool: Finding Your Ikigai

What is your reason for living? Finding your life's purpose isn't something to be rushed; it is something to be constantly pursuing until it is found. These questions are a starting point for finding your Ikigai.

List as many things as possible that bring a smile when you think about them. Don't try to rationalize; just brainstorm (for example, dogs, my kids, reading, surfing):

_____

_____

_____

_____

_____

_____

What unique talents or gifts do you bring to the world? What is your unique superpower? How do you use this superpower to make the world a better place?

_____

_____

_____

_____

_____

_____

Who are the people who are the most meaningful to you? Interactions with these individuals should leave you feeling recharged and energetic rather than drained:

_____

_____

_____

_____

_____

Are there any locations you feel a calling to visit or live in? What is it about these locations that interests you? What would be your ideal?

_____

_____

_____

_____

(*continued*)

(continued)

_____

_____

What industries or professions interest you the most? Why?

_____

_____

_____

_____

_____

_____

What is your heart telling you? Close your eyes and
imagine achieving a state of self-realization. What is
the ultimate fulfillment of your potential?

_____

_____

_____

_____

_____

_____

_____

_____

_____

_____

_____

_____

17

Vision, Mission, and Values

Everyone within an organization should understand the company's vision, mission, and core values. Without clarity on these three things, it's almost impossible to reach an organization's full potential. Let's start by clarifying what each of these is and why they are all essential.

- A company vision is why an organization exists. This is the business's WHY statement. One of the best examples of a company's *why* statement is Apple's company vision, which is to build the best products in the world that enrich people's lives.

- Strategic missions are the short-term objectives that align with the overarching company vision. These short-term goals are typically 90-day initiatives that are steps toward achieving the company vision.

- Core values are fundamental for an organization for many reasons. They are a decision-making tool that can be applied by every employee, from the CEO to the person dealing directly with customers. Core values are better than standard operating procedures (SOPs), which do not allow for the unique circumstances that will arise within an organization.

Clarifying the Vision

The vision is the organization's future state. In most cases, the company's vision is ambitious, if not a BHAG (Big Hairy Audacious Goal). It clearly states the organization's purpose and the impact it will have on the people it was created to serve. In stating the vision, we want to communicate the reason *why* the organization exists and inspire others to embrace the shared goal. Working toward a goal that your team is passionate about is more inspiring than financial reward. Having a shared vision in an organization is the galvanizing effect required to accomplish extraordinary things. The world's best and brightest have choices in where they spend their time and who they choose to work with. Financial compensation is no longer the most essential ingredient in the recipe for having an exceptional team.

The vision serves as the organization's guiding North Star. For example, Feed the Children's vision is to create a world where no child goes hungry. That is a powerful goal that will inspire exceptional people to help take on this enormous global challenge because it's such an important cause that everyone cares about.

Define your vision and create a clear and concise statement that conveys the organization's "why." Once you have the vision defined, shout it from the rooftops. It should be on the homepage of the website, in every job posting, and even in the art that hangs on the wall of the offices. Most importantly, the vision should be shared and embraced by everyone.

Defining the Mission

The mission statement defines what the organization is currently working on. The vision is typically so broad and represents a future state that will require creating a long-term plan broken down into individual short-term "missions" to accomplish.

I like breaking the missions into yearly themes that consist of four quarterly goals that together are the most important initiatives that will have the highest impact. Those quarterly goals are owned by an individual team member who reports on the status weekly to make sure the initiative is on track, and if not, the organization can help remove obstacles or add the resources required. The person who owns the goal is not required to do all the work alone, but they are responsible for its completion. When more than one person owns something, nobody is truly accountable.

Figuring Out Your Business's Core Values

Most businesses today have core values. Are they the right values? When done well, core values serve as a guiding star for an organization. They also serve as guardrails to keep the company on its path, keeping it from losing direction through a series of decisions made without clarity of vision. Every choice someone makes within the company can use the core values as a decision-making filter to help them make the right decision for the customer and the company. For this to work, the values have to be authentic.

Too many companies have what I would refer to as "table stakes" core values. They are either the minimum required values, or they are generalizations. For example, the idea of "do the right thing" should apply to all business and personal interactions, but that is precisely why it's too vague to be a guiding principle.

There is a phenomenal tool to help identify the fundamental core values of any company. For best results, use a moderator who is not an employee to facilitate the session. Have your leadership team each select two or three of their favorite co-workers. I am a fan of having everyone write them on sticky notes individually to avoid groupthink, and once the team has made their selections, collectively put them on the whiteboard. Inevitably, there will be certain team members whose names will end up on the board multiple times.

Once everyone has shared their favorite co-workers, the magic happens. Start with the name that has the most sticky notes on the wall; in this example, we will use "Tomas" as our star teammate. Have everyone who chose Tomas as one of their favorites share the reasons why they selected him. Write down all of the reasons on the whiteboard. Tomas is process driven, he can solve any problem and will create an SOP with the process he creates, he is incredibly detail oriented, and on and on. As you go around the room, certain themes will emerge across the chosen "favorites."

The next step is to craft these consistent themes into values. In the agency, the process was something that set us apart from the competition, creating a better customer experience and enabling the team to deliver exceptional work consistently. Our core value was "Process Gurus." It accomplished two things. First, it simplified the complex projects we worked on and broke them down into a step-by-step playbook that we could apply to every client. Second, the process was communicated to the client before they ever signed the contract to work with us. For many of our customers, it was the core value of "Process Guru" that resonated with them when they were selecting the right agency for their project.

Have a definition of each value that can be explained simply by anyone in the organization AND know examples of how the organization authentically lives them. In addition to Process Gurus, my agency also had the following core values:

- Quantitative Creativity
- Perpetual Karma
- Reputation Guardians
- Industry Innovators

Quantitative Creativity was an incredible differentiator from our competition. Most agencies are excellent at spinning the analytics to show positive results. It could be traffic on the website, impressions of ads in front of potential customers, or any multitude of metrics. We prided ourselves on having a single number that the customer held us accountable to, and ideally it had a dollar sign in front of it. We measured the amount of revenue a company experiences due to our efforts. In many instances, it's not definitive where a sale came from since the buyer has been exposed to the brand in a variety of ways, from driving the right target audience to the website via paid ads, to social media influence, ongoing email marketing, geofencing advertising, retargeting ads, or optimizing the website to capture leads and increase conversion. Even when we couldn't break down the influence of each channel that converted the prospect to a client, we could always attribute the revenue to activities. Our clients could hold us accountable for the results or lack thereof.

The core value of Perpetual Karma came from my Buddhist beliefs. We applied the same Karma to business relationships that I applied in my personal life. Many times we far exceeded what would have qualified as "do the right thing" to make sure a customer was taken care of. Our clients and employees would always act ethically and with compassion even in the most stressful business situations.

Zenman was one of the only agencies that maintained a five-star rating online. Reputation Guardians meant that we made sure we did the right thing *when* something went wrong. Notice I used the word *when* and not *if* something goes wrong. In any business, eventually a client will experience a problem with your product or service, and how you deal with it is the difference between an exceptional reputation with raving fans for customers or a permanent blemish on your brand.

The final value of Industry Innovators feels like it could be applied to most agencies; however, I kept this value because our team was constantly pushing the boundaries in our industry, so it did ring true.

Determining Personal Core Values

I have a different technique for finding your personal core values at the end of this chapter. The cool thing about this exercise is that it works at any age, because the values that matter to us are established very early.

Start by contemplating who your hero is. It can be one or two people, and they could even be fictional characters. Once you have identified your hero, list the characteristics that led you to select them out of the eight billion people on the planet. Try to identify four to five reasons and clearly state them.

My personal core values are Leadership, Fatherhood, Laughter, Creativity, and Adventure. The one that has evolved later in life is "Fatherhood," which was family for me before I became a dad. Nothing in my experience has clarified what my true responsibility is in this lifetime like the birth of my first son. Before that, I had felt responsible for my family and friends, causing me to carry the burden of that incorrect assumption for most of my life.

Tool: Core Values

What are your personal core values? Do you know what truly drives you? Many of us try to define our values but default to what we think society expects of us. This tool helps determine the core values that are the most important to you. It can be done at any age and is an exceptional tool for families to help come up with their collective values and the values of each individual.

Who is your hero? It could be a historical figure, a family member, or even a fictional character like Superman.

_____

_____

Why are they your hero?

_____

_____

_____

_____

_____

_____

_____

_____

_____

_____

_____

_____

_____

_____

(continued)

(continued)

_____

_____

_____

*Distill the things you admire about your hero and craft them into
your core values. For example, if you selected your grandmother
as your hero and in the Reasons Why that she overcame tremendous adversity in her life by doing whatever was necessary for her
family, one of your values would be "Do Whatever It Takes."*

Core Value: _____

_____

_____

Core Value: _____

_____

_____

Core Value: _____

_____

_____

Core Value: _____

_____

_____

Core Value: _____

_____

_____

Mind (*samadhi*)

"There is no path to happiness: happiness is the path."

—Buddha

CHAPTER

18

Right Effort

Right Effort is presented as "The monk arouses his will, puts forth effort, generates energy, exerts his mind, and strives to prevent the arising of evil and unwholesome mental states that have not yet arisen." To live life to its full potential, we must put forth the Right Effort.

Through continuous growth and self-exploration, we make incremental progress. We can't just wait around with good intentions and expect our lives to be complete. Right Effort refers to everything we do, from our work to how we show up in our relationships and friendships and in doing life's most trivial tasks. How you do anything is how you do everything.

A Few Principles of Right Effort

You know the path, but sometimes doing the right thing isn't easy. This is actually the time we need to be most mindful of making the Right Effort. Many times, the easy path is the wrong path, or doing the right thing might result in an uncomfortable conversation or conflict. In my experience, if we are struggling with something in our lives, it usually means that a difficult conversation has been avoided or has not been handled well.

Right Effort also means that you have shown up and are 100 percent ready to take on the task at hand. One of the most pointed insights I have ever heard was "Nerves mean you care; fear means you are unprepared. Be nervous, not afraid." When you have thoroughly prepared for the journey in front of you, the feeling of nervousness can become exhilarating. Part of being prepared means showing up in the best state possible to overcome the challenges we face each day. How we show up can easily mean the difference between success and failure. Sometimes that means taking time out to prioritize self-care for our mind and body.

Once upon a time, but not so long ago that it's not still relevant now, there lived two lumberjacks. Every day they would eat their flapjacks or whatever breakfast a lumberjack ate and head into the forest together. All morning, the two men worked side by side, cutting down trees and chopping them into piles of lumber. The first lumberjack would take a short break to eat lunch and work until sunset. The second man would return home for a couple of hours and resume work mid-afternoon for a couple of hours, consistently finishing in time to watch the sunset on the horizon, much to the chagrin of the man who labored endlessly yet produced significantly less lumber

> Kaizen *is the concept of focusing on minor improvements every day because it's impossible to change overnight. Never fall into the trap of comparing yourself to others; the only comparison that matters is this: Are you 1 percent better than you were yesterday?*

every day. After years of trying to outwork his peer, the first man finally broke down and proclaimed in anger, "How is it that every day I work from dusk to dawn chopping wood while you stop each day for hours to do who knows what, and yet you still outpace me? What do you do every day when you are at home, and I am busting my ass chopping wood?!" Calmly, the second lumberjack replied, "When I go home, I eat, rest my mind and body, and sharpen my axe."

Right Effort in Business

I learned the hard way how painful it can be when you cut corners. This is going to age me, but I went to Brooks Institute of Photography in the early 1990s and studied commercial and undersea photography. The way the program worked was that each week we would get a new assignment that would be presented the following class and we would be critiqued for the previous week's work. This critique was not only from the professor but also from our peers. Critiques were painful. It was not uncommon for tears to be shed.

One of the things that set Brooks Institute apart from the competition in those days was how hard it was actually to graduate with a degree from this school. At Brooks, a C was a failing grade; if you received two Cs, you flunked out of school. That was it, no second chances. Of the 50-plus people who started in my class, just over a dozen of us graduated.

The bar was so high to pass that most weeks we would receive our new assignment and fail the previous week's project, receiving a redo. Again, I'm aging myself here, but back in my day we shot on film, processed everything by hand—including spooling the 35 mm film onto the processing reel in pitch black—and then printed in a dark room dimly lit with a red light that wouldn't fog the photographic paper, followed by hand retouching any prints before finally dry-mounting the print on a presentation board. I remember this morning like it was yesterday; I had been working through the night to finish a print for critique. This photograph required not only a lot of complicated dodging and burning throughout the darkroom printing process, but also needed hand retouching, which was painstakingly slow. I was up all night retouching this photo, and the following day the print was barely dry, leaving me no time to dry-mount it for the presentation. Instead, I cut the very last corner and spray-mounted the print, thinking, "It would be impossible to tell the difference."

This class started out spectacularly well. I recall receiving the most positive feedback from my peers of any critique since I had started at Brooks. Dave Litchell was my professor, and I remember he walked up to the front of the class where all of the prints were mounted and displayed. He took mine off the wall and showered me with compliments about the photograph, composition, and the quality of the finished print. Then he did something I will never forget. He flexed the presentation board, creating enough of a bend, which made my spray-mounted print begin to dismount ever so slightly from the presentation board. Dave then grabbed the corner of my print, slowly peeled it off the board, crumbling it up, and before he threw it at me, said, "Next time, follow directions."

Sometimes the best lessons we learn in life are the hardest to experience in the moment. Dave is still one of my all-time favorite teachers, and a lesson he taught me that day was transformational. Right Effort means taking the time to do things to the best of your ability.

Dependability and consistency are indispensable in building a business. Starbucks is the perfect example of consistency over exceptional. Starbucks is the world's largest coffee brand in total sales ($32.3 billion in 2022) as well as number of stores (over 35,000 in 80 countries), and it was built by replicating the same quality product and experience no matter which location you get your coffee. Personally, it's not my favorite coffee. However, they are reliable in delivering the same burnt-tasting java in every Starbucks around the world. Several factors contributed to the success, including making coffee a cultural experience that offers a level of social status for its patrons. However, the reason someone would pay $9 for a Venti Caffé Latte with an extra shot and endless options of additional accoutrements is that they can depend on the uniformity of the experience.

It takes less time to do something right the first time than to revisit a task that should have already been completed. Famed basketball coach John Wooden said, "If you don't have time to do it right, when will you have time to do it over?" Nothing could have been more accurate when it came to redoing my print in college, and it translates into our professional lives. In a landscape where most of us are operating from a place of constant distractions, it's becoming increasingly harder to deliver our best work.

Slow down to speed up. Taking our time and having Right Concentration (see Chapter 22) results in more efficiency and higher quality. Studies consistently find that teams that take a slower, more methodical approach achieve results more quickly. That does not mean to work aimlessly or recklessly. Some people have the approach "ready—aim—aim—aim—aim—fire," while others take more of a "fire-ready-aim" approach. Similar to the Middle Way, there is an art to understanding when enough information is available to make an informed decision. Ideally, this results in a "ready—aim—fire" cadence. This means allowing enough time to be taken to have clarity and direction without missing the window of opportunity.

Consistency in Your Right Effort

The topic of consistency is touched on as a component of many aspects of the Noble Eightfold Path. This is due to the fact that it is fundamentally one of the two most essential traits for success (the other is Clarity of Vision, introduced in Chapter 5). Brazilian novelist Paulo Coelho said, "The distance between dreams and reality is called discipline."

Discipline does not mean showing up perfectly every single day—quite the opposite. It means showing up on the days when we're struggling and hardly have anything to give, but we show up anyway. Realistic expectations help us with our willpower and consistent discipline. If you expect to see significant progress through short bursts of extreme effort, you're kidding yourself. The small things we do add up over time but have the most profound compound result imaginable.

There is a misconception that individuals need to focus on their personal brand, and nothing is further from the truth. Focus on keeping your commitments, delivering what you said when you said you would, and always achieving the best possible quality while being professional and pleasant in the process. The need to "brand" yourself disappears when you establish a reputation for consistently delivering on your word.

> *I fear not the man who practiced 10,000 kicks once, but I fear the man who has practiced one kick 10,000 times.*
>
> —*Bruce Lee*

Tool: Creating Balance and Momentum

Efforts should be focused on the areas that need it the most. Identify the eight areas of focus that matter in your life, such as Mindfulness, Physical Health, Relationships, and so on. Plot them on the wheel in Figure 18.1, then score each one on a scale of 1–10.

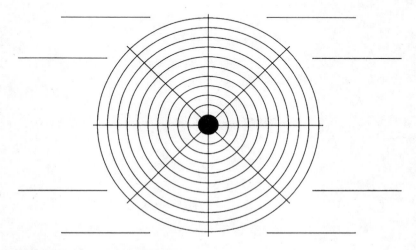

FIGURE 18.1 Identifying your areas of focus.

Source: Keith Roberts

Based on your answers, is the wheel balanced? What areas need improvement, and what are the next steps to balancing this wheel so you can gain momentum? Remember, they don't all have to be at a 10; balance is more important. We don't want a few at 7, 8, and 9, while other areas you identified as critical are 3, 4, or 5.

_____

_____

_____

19

Misogi

In today's world, we have become much softer than ever before in human history. It's not healthy to be constantly heated or air conditioned to the ideal temperature while effortlessly ordering groceries to be delivered to our doorstep. Believe it or not, it's not only healthy but is actually essential to push ourselves to our limits from time to time—something that most of the world today never experiences.

Part of Right Effort is truly giving something 100 percent of our ability and truly finding the limits of what we are capable of. One way to find our limits is traditional Misogi, an ancient Japanese practice originating from the Shinto tradition. Central to the Shinto belief is the concept of purification, both physically and spiritually. Misogi is a ritual within this ancient tradition aimed at cleansing the mind, body, and spirit.

A Little Misogi History

The history of Misogi dates back to the tale of Izanagi and his wife, Izanami. When Izanami died and descended into Yomi (the land of the dead), Izanagi was overwhelmed with grief and refused to accept her fate. He ventured into Yomi and finally found his beloved wife, who asked him not to look at her, but he lit a torch and saw her decomposing body. Izanagi stumbled back in disgust, revealing himself to the spirits of Yomi. Izanami was enraged and sent the demons after him. Izanagi fought his way back to the boundary between Yomi and the living world and covered the entrance with a large boulder, sealing the spirits inside. Upon reaching the land of the living, he discovered that his own body had begun to decay as a consequence of his time in Yomi, and he cleansed himself in cold waters, washing every part of his body. Afterward, he felt a purification and reenergization in his life.

The traditional Misogi typically occurs under a sacred waterfall, lake, or river. In the original tradition, the participants would undergo a preliminary cleansing that could involve fasting, prayer, and mental or physical challenges. One of the most profound places to experience the Misogi is the Nachi Waterfall in Japan. The staggering 133-meter falls have been a sacred pilgrimage for centuries, and practitioners continue immersing themselves in the icy waters to cleanse their minds, body, and spirit.

This is evolving in the West into a yearly tradition that someone undertakes to push themselves to the limit and grow exponentially in the process. It is a challenge that pushes us to our limits and forces us to confront our doubts, weaknesses, and fears about what we are truly capable of. Long gone are the days when we really had to push ourselves to survive—humans have become soft compared to our ancestors a few hundred years ago. We need to remind ourselves what is truly possible when we push ourselves to the limit. That's why working out with a trainer is so much more impactful than working out on your own. The trainer knows how much more is possible when you think, "I've done enough," and they will push you harder than you push yourself, which causes faster growth (in this case, of muscles or stamina). A Misogi does the same thing.

My friend Jimmy May was a Navy SEAL. He told me that when most of us think we have nothing left in the tank, we've actually given only 40 percent. Think about that! When most people give up, we still have 60 percent left in our reserves. When you push past the point that you think is your limit, it taps into an incredible unrealized reserve.

The Two Rules of a Misogi

A Misogi pushes us to our limit, but the only way we can actually know our limit is to reach it. Once a year, craft a challenge that really pushes you to find what you are capable of—something that gets you out of your comfort zone and allows you to test yourself in ways modern society no longer does.

There are a few things to know before attempting your first Misogi. Call them the two rules of a misogi:

1. Don't die.
2. You should fail at least half the time.

The first rule might sound extreme or even off-putting, but it is also imperative. Depending on the physical challenge you are attempting, it is conceivable to end up tired, lost, or even unconscious in potentially life-threatening situations. I know a couple of guys who tried to paddleboard from Santa Barbara to the Channel Islands. That is 30 miles of open ocean, and without a support crew on a boat to ensure their safety while failing, Misogi would have almost certainly ended in tragedy.

Why is the second rule "You should fail at least half the time"? Simply put, if you succeed in all of your attempts to push to the limits of what's possible, you will never find your most significant potential. I'll give you an example. If you had to carry 250 pounds for a mile, do you think it's possible? It's inconceivable to me right now that I could sustain carrying a fraction of that weight for that distance. But what if it was a close friend who was wounded on the battlefield? How far could you carry that weight if a loved one's life depended on it? We don't know what we are actually capable of until we test ourselves. When you find your actual breaking point, it's miles past what was previously unimaginable.

My first Misogi attempt was to carry a rock a mile underwater. Not in one breath, obviously, but rather in the same way big wave surfers train to hold their breath for prolonged periods of time. The attempt took place in the warm waters of Costa Rica, which had exceptional visibility and almost zero surf on the day. To give myself the highest possible chance of success, I used a kettlebell that would be easy to grab with a dive glow stick so that I could readily see it. I carried the kettlebell until my head was underwater and walked about 10 yards before surfacing for a breath. I failed tremendously, barely able to make it a quarter mile before I thought I was going to drown and had to be helped to shore, but I made it much farther than I thought possible before the attempt.

What would your first Misogi be? Really push yourself and remember the Navy SEAL 40 percent rule: If you're setting a goal that you think is your limit for your first Misogi, double it. What a gift it would be for you to actually find your physical and mental limit on your first attempt. Choose an activity you are passionate about or something that has always intimidated you. Maybe there's travel involved, or it could be part of a sacred pilgrimage. This is a once-in-a-year opportunity to have a profound transformational and purification experience that teaches us what we're really capable of accomplishing it. Embrace this opportunity. Without understanding what our limits are, most of us will consistently live in a world far below what we're capable of.

Tool: Misogi Roadmap

Each year, we should all undertake a Misogi to find our personal limits. By pushing ourselves, we find out what we are truly capable of accomplishing. It's incredibly freeing to know that you are going to come up short of your goal at least half the time. Many new Misogi practitioners find that they successfully complete the first few attempts because they genuinely didn't realize what they are capable of accomplishing.

When planning your Misogi, remember the two rules:

1. *Don't die.*

2. *You should fail at least half the time.*

A Misogi is NOT an extreme sport or an activity that risks your life like running with the bulls. It is a physical challenge that pushes you to your individual limits.

Create the roadmap for your next Misogi by answering the following questions:

What have you always wanted to try but have been hesitant to attempt for fear of failure?

_____

_____

_____

(continued)

(*continued*)

_____

_____

_____

Is there a location that has sacred meaning or that has been calling you to visit?

_____

_____

_____

_____

_____

_____

Think about books you have read or stories that inspired you. What are some of the physical challenges that have interested you?

_____

_____

_____

_____

_____

State the Misogi you will attempt in the next year. Start with the future date for the attempt and describe what successfully completing the Misogi will look like. What is the physical challenge you will attempt? Clearly state your goal and what success looks like.

_____

_____

_____

_____

_____

_____

Required safety precautions: How are you going to ensure safety in this attempt? Who will be your safety person? Is any equipment necessary? Are there seasonal considerations that could impact safety due to weather conditions?

_____

_____

_____

_____

_____

CHAPTER

20

Right Mindfulness

In the Noble Eightfold Path, Right Mindfulness helps us not to crave or cling to any temporary state or transient thing. It is maintaining a positive state without letting weaker, unwholesome thoughts take root in our subconscious. Practicing Right Mindfulness means we are fully present in our bodies, thoughts, and senses.

Mindfulness is not associated with any specific religious doctrines, although it is embraced in many spiritual practices. This means that practicing mindfulness will not go against your existing religious beliefs.

Mindfulness is the practice of slowing down and focusing on the present moment. It can be achieved through various practices, such as focusing on your breath, scanning your body, yoga, and even mindful eating. The most common way to practice Right Mindfulness is through meditation.

In Zen Buddhism, we practice mindfulness at all times. While doing anything from driving a car to writing a proposal for work, the goal is to be completely present and solely focused on a single object or task. The reality is that thoughts constantly interrupt us, but the trick is to become aware that your focus has shifted, pause, then go back to solely focus.

Achieving Mindfulness with Meditation

Meditation helps attain Right Mindfulness, allowing us to experience the present moment without distraction, but it also does so much more. Meditation is proven to reduce anxiety, depression, and even physical fatigue. Mindfulness also benefits our memory, creativity, and problem-solving skills, along with increased focus. If that's not enough, studies have also shown a better reduction in physical pain through meditation compared to pharmaceuticals and it has been transformational in helping veterans with PTSD.

The four foundation of mindfulness are Kāyā, Vedanā, Citta, and Dhamma.

- **Kāyā—Activities of the body:** Mindfulness around our body requires starting with our breath, posture, and throughout the day's activities. From eating our food to taking a shower, we are present and singularly focused on the moment we are currently experiencing.

- **Vedanā—Feelings or sensations:** Mindfulness of our feelings means we can categorize them as either pleasant, neutral, or unpleasant. Our awareness of how we initially react provides insights into the work we still need to do. Vedanā reveals fear, ego, or unhealthy desires, allowing us to recognize and release those feelings.

- **Citta—Activities of the heart and mind:** Citta refers to the emotions we feel that come from our heart and mind. Become aware of the presence of the any of the three poisons—hate, delusion, and greed. Acknowledge and release them because they do not serve you.

- **Dhamma—Ideas and thoughts:** The fourth foundation is the reflection of Buddha's teaching. The five groups specifically mentioned are:

  - The Five Hindrances (sensual desire, ill-will, sloth, restlessness, doubt)
  - The Five Aggregates (form, feeling, perceptions, formations, consciousness)
  - The Six Pairs of Sense Bases (eye, ear, nose, tongue, body, mind)
  - The Seven Factors of Enlightenment (mindfulness, investigation, energy, rapture, tranquility, concentration, equanimity)
  - The Four Noble Truths (life is suffering, cause of suffering, cessation of suffering, path to end suffering)

Mindfulness is achieved in part through meditation. Psychologist C. George Boeree wrote, "Buddhism began by encouraging its practitioners to engage in (sati) or mindfulness, that is, developing a full consciousness of all about you and within you—whether seated in a special posture or simply going about one's life. This is the kind of meditation that Buddha himself engaged in under the bodhi tree."

Meditation is the most common practice among the world's happiest and highest-performing humans. It's a practical way to see more. If someone says they don't have time for meditation, they need some form of mindfulness more than anyone. If you think you don't have time to meditate, I promise the practice actually gives you back time. By clearing our minds and being able to focus without distraction, we're more creative and productive.

Meditation also has incredible benefits for those around us, beyond just experiencing us in a more awakened state. There's a study called the Maharishi effect, which was first investigated in the early 1970s when American cities that had at least a 1 percent population that practiced Transcendental Meditation saw a significant crime reduction. To test this, in 1993 the Transcendental Meditation community went to Washington, DC, with 4,000 TM practitioners, and during the time they practiced Transcendental Meditation, Washington, DC, saw a decrease of 23 percent in violent crime. It benefits not only the practitioner but also those around us.

If you think the benefits are impressive for those not practicing meditation, imagine the results it has for the person actually meditating. Studies have shown the benefits of meditation include reducing stress, getting better sleep, lowering blood pressure, improving cognitive abilities to solve complex problems, increasing emotional intelligence, increasing focus, enabling better memory, and even helping with trauma and PTSD.

One of the most exciting results in recent studies is the ongoing state of gamma brain waves that consistent meditation practitioners experience. Gamma brain waves are associated with a high level of consciousness and can be experienced when one is intensely focused, highly present in the moment, or in a state of fascination. The most advanced meditators are in an almost constant state of gamma brain waves.

The other magical thing about meditation is that you can't do it wrong. Most people struggle with meditation, whether they're trying a guided meditation, a contemplative meditation technique, or a concentrated meditation. The struggle that most people experience is that while they're meditating, they find that thoughts are entering their minds. I promise you this happens to even the most advanced meditators.

My favorite form of meditation is Transcendental Meditation, otherwise known as TM. The wonderful thing about this practice is that it teaches you right up front that you can't do it wrong. You learn a mantra that you repeat over and over in your mind for 15–20 minutes, and while you're thinking this word that has no meaning at any pace while you breathe in and out, your mind eventually reaches a transcended state where it's at peace with itself. You're not thinking about anything else at all. It's pure euphoria for our mind, and it lasts for a very brief instant. And then, as soon as you realize you've stopped thinking about your mantra and you've gone back to worrying about that proposal that had to get sent out, all you have to do is go back to that mantra and eventually return to that transcendental state.

Whatever type of meditation calls to you is perfect. There's no excuse to say you don't know how to meditate with all of the existing options, from exceptional meditation apps on our phones to local meetups and even a library of free online video recordings of guided meditations.

Right Mindfulness in Business

From Silicon Valley giants like Steve Jobs to creatives like Jerry Seinfeld, Oprah Winfrey, and even Howard Stern, many very successful people attribute large parts of their success to their meditation practice. Oprah introduced Transcendental Meditation to her staff at Harpo Studios in the early 2000s. She eventually paid for all 400 employees to take the Transcendental Meditation course. It became part of their daily structure that all employees meditated together at 9:00 in the morning and again at 4:30 in the afternoon. Oprah said, "No matter what is going on, we stop and meditate."

Mindfulness in the workplace means being consciously present. When everyone is focused on a single thing, whether it's the email they are composing or paying attention to the person speaking in a meeting, the results are quantifiably better. Distractions kill creativity. Remove laptops, phones, and tablets from meetings and go tech-free for the brief time everyone is in a room together. Eliminate the distraction of checking emails or responding to messages by not having a laptop open during a meeting. This will increase engagement significantly, boosting the efficiency and output of meetings while simultaneously removing the barriers that are separating our team and will help build bonds.

The benefits of meditation and mindfulness at work are immense, ranging from increased motivation and improved problem-solving, to reduced stress, enhanced memory, and cultivating harmonious relationships through increased connection and compassion. And those are just the benefits at the office. Employees who practice mindfulness will also see benefits in their personal happiness and relationships.

Giving your team the tools and culture that embrace mindfulness in the workplace will reduce conflict, create better interactions between employees and customers, improve focus, and ultimately increase output while maintaining or leveling up quality. The bottom line is that meditation makes not only the individual but also the organization better.

Why do I meditate? To bring clarity to my life.

Mediation brings wisdom, lack of mediation leaves ignorance. Know well what leads you forward and what holds you back, and choose the path that leads to wisdom.

—Buddha

Tool: Meditation and Results

Schedule 15 minutes in your morning routine for mindfulness. Queue one of the free guided meditations at http://www .zenman.com/meditations *and hit play. Start by closing your eyes and breathing deeply through your nose and exhalating through the mouth.*

What was that experience like? Did you reach a state where your mind wasn't thinking about your responsibilities? What ideas came to you during the meditation? Capture them now to take action on them.

_____

_____

_____

_____

_____

_____

_____

_____

_____

_____

_____

_____

_____

21

The Law of Attraction

The Law of Attraction works for us and against us. Right Mindfulness (see Chapter 20) is vital to ensure we are attracting the proper type of energy into our lives. If we have an abundant mindset, we will attract that same vibration back to us and receive abundance. If our mindset is that of scarcity, we will receive scarcity in return. We must be intentional with the thoughts and words we use about ourselves. They are powerful and are shaping our future.

"I am" are the most powerful two words in any language. They are a declaration made to the universe about a future state that will come to fruition. These powerful words can be used to manifest dreams into reality or to attract heartbreak into our lives. Writing down your "I am" declaration doubles the probability of reaching the goal. Writing *"The Zen of Business* is a *New York Times* Best Seller" is putting that energy out into the universe, giving it an opportunity to become a reality.

My poker buddies say I'm the luckiest guy in the world and have been playing hold 'em with me for the last two decades. I genuinely believe that, in addition to being an exceptional poker player with a knack for reading people, I can manifest cards. I play to win, not to lose. That said, I don't win every time, but if I keep score over a year, I'm consistently up. I also have a couple of friends who have a scarcity mindset, and it's truly mind-boggling how powerfully they can manifest consistent catastrophic events in their lives that you couldn't imagine happening in fiction.

Embracing the Law of Attraction

There are actually techniques you can use to harness the power of the Law of Attraction. The first one is simple, and the benefits are tremendous. Practice gratitude. When we're grateful, it attends to our frequency in abundance. Vision boards and positive affirmations are other tools that help with planting the seeds of our future and watering them consistently until they bloom. The "Visualizing the Future" tool used at the end of Chapter 2 was planting those seeds for living your best life, and the remaining chapters have been the water, food, and sunlight for your soul.

Jim Carrey is my favorite example of visualizing the desired outcome and working hard toward achieving it. In November 1988, Jim wrote himself a check for $10,000,000 and put in the memo "Acting Services Rendered." He postdated the check for three years in the future. It ended up taking him 10 years, but in November 1998, Jim Carrey was paid $10 million for arguably the best role in cinema history: Lloyd in *Dumb and Dumber*. But Carrey didn't sit around for years waiting for opportunities to fall in his lap. He worked his butt off in everything from *In Living Color* to literally talking with his ass cheeks in *Ace Ventura*. He visualized his future and then spent the next 10 years building it. In fact, he famously said, "Visualization works if you do the hard work. That's the thing. You can't just visualize and go eat a sandwich."

That story also illustrates how humans overestimate what is possible to accomplish in a year, but we underestimate what can be done in a decade. When we set goals without actually allowing enough time to accomplish them, it can be discouraging. Patience is the most overlooked discipline required to achieve great things. Whether we are working to scale a business or trying to improve our physical health through diet and exercise, results take time.

Setting intentions creates an invisible path to reaching your goal. The ability to achieve goals depends on three things: our diet, a trusted circle, and our habits.

- **Our diet:** This does not only refer to the food that we put into our bodies; it's also the content we digest. Let's start with the fuel that we feed our bodies. Think of what we eat and drink as fuel for the one body we get in this life. Nourish yourself with healthy food while avoiding toxins as much as possible. Be as thoughtful with the content we feed our brains as we are with the food we put in our bodies. Remember the Middle Way and avoid extremes when it comes to any content, whether it is news, social media, or binge-watching Netflix.

- **Trusted circle:** You are the sum of the five people you spend the most time with. If you are the smartest person in the room, you are in the wrong room. Always be seeking to grow while continuing to be the teacher when the time is right.

- **Our habits:** Our habits add up to become our future, so be mindful of your routines. What we are doing now is a mirror of the results we can expect. Cultivating healthy habits while eliminating detrimental ones will result in incremental growth that will compound over time.

The Law of Attraction works only if you do the work. Surround yourself with people who push you to grow and make continuous progress every day. Maintain that clarity of vision and continuous daily progress. If you do this, there is nothing you can't accomplish.

The Law of Attraction in Business

The Law of Attraction in business works the same way. Start by clearly stating the organization's goals and physically write them down. Be very Yoda about how you state all the objectives: "Do or do not, there is no try." Set specific goals that align with the shared vision and communicate them often using the "I am" approach. Always align the messaging from a place of Right Thought (see Chapter 8). Nobody is motivated by leaders who come across as consistently negative.

- **Set specific goals:** When writing an organization's goal, whether it's a BHAG or a quarterly initiative, be as specific as possible while including all necessary details. Don't set a vague sales goal of "significant growth." Be exact with the percent of growth and the actual dollar amount of the goal. Break that down into a scorecard or KPI that can track the progress along the way.

- **Be intentional with how you speak:** Speak with confidence. It's vital that this belief is genuine. Clients, prospects, and employees can sense inauthenticity or a scarcity mindset. Be honest, but also believe in your abilities to do great things.

- **Remind them of *why* (the vision):** Frequently communicate the reason it's important for the organization to achieve its vision. Sharing the *why* inspires the people working hard to reach the goal while attracting the customers it serves.

Positive thinking and hard work will attract the right employees and the right customers. The secret is that it is equal parts mindset and consistent effort.

Tool: "I Am" Mantras

*I and **am** are the two most powerful words in any language. Nine is a powerful number in manifesting because it signifies inner rebirth and transformation into our best possible self. Write three sets of "I am" affirmations: one for business, another for relationships, and the last for yourself.*

Business

I am _____

I am _____

I am _____

I am _____

I am _____

I am _____

I am _____

I am _____

I am _____

Relationships

I am _____

I am _____

I am _____

I am _____

I am _____

(continued)

(*continued*)

I am _____

I am _____

I am _____

I am _____

Personal

I am _____

I am _____

I am _____

I am _____

I am _____

I am _____

I am _____

I am _____

I am _____

CHAPTER

22

Right Concentration

Focusing all of our attention on one object or theme is Right Concentration. In this settled state, we can see things as they indeed are without being clouded by greed, envy, or other ill thoughts. Right Concentration is the ability to stay focused on a single thing without the mind wandering.

Be aware of where you are focusing your energy and intention. Our thoughts create impressions that are seeds in our minds, which I've discussed many times throughout this book. Plant the seeds you want to grow in the garden of your life. If you think about adverse events or worry about the future, you're actually putting out into the universe a frequency to attract precisely that which you are trying to avoid.

It might seem counterintuitive, but worrying about a potential problem is the absolute worst possible thing you can do about it. First, by focusing energy on a potential issue, we are actually increasing the likelihood of manifesting that very problem.

The impermanence of this world is challenging enough that we don't need to focus on creating more suffering in life. Secondly, worrying does absolutely no good. If there is something that you are concerned with, make sure you have done everything in your power to address the concern. If you haven't, don't waste your time worrying; do the work. If you have done everything within your power to address the concern, there is no need to worry because the outcome is out of your control.

When bad things happen, have the right mindset to minimize your suffering. If there's one thing that's certain, we will all experience challenging times. There's a Buddhist fable of the two arrows in dealing with suffering. Buddha says that anytime we suffer misfortune, two arrows fly our way. Being struck by the first arrow is painful. Being struck by a second arrow is even worse. Buddha explained, "In life, we can't always control the first arrow. However, the second arrow is our reaction to the first. The second arrow is optional."

Where our thoughts go, our energy flows. Take your time in deciding your intentions, and be mindful that the future you imagine will generate focus, which translates into energy, which will equal results. Be intentional with how you view your future because the universe will say "yes."

I have a process when setting goals to help increase the chance of achieving them. I start with having a mantra or concise statement using the "I am" method (see Chapter 21). For example, "I am a *New York Times* best-selling author." Once you have the mantra, the next step is to close your eyes and paint a clear picture in your mind of that goal being reached. Finally, and most importantly, with the mantra in your mind and an image you can see, the last step is to actually *feel* what it's like to reach the goal. Have a mantra, see the goal, and feel it. These three steps will make you unstoppable.

Right Concentration in Business

Right Concentration in business often means staying focused on the vision and mission (see Chapter 17). An entrepreneur's greatest strength and uttermost weakness is their ability to come up with new ideas. Having ideas isn't actually the hard part of business; the real challenge is executing them. That battle only continues to spiral as a business grows and the founder continuously comes up with new innovations that distract from the one thing they originally set out to do. The ability to remain focused on the mission until it's completed is the difference between consistent success and frequent disappointment.

Right Concentration in business means taking off our rose-colored glasses and seeing things as they truly are. At times it can be challenging or even disheartening to take an unbiased look at a situation and make the best decision with the information available at the time. I am an eternal optimist when it comes to what is possible, and at the same time, decades of running an agency left scars and calluses along the way. The lesson that took me the longest to learn in business is to be realistic. Never make plans based on best-case scenarios. It's much easier to adjust when things go better than expected versus trying to correct course when we fall short of our goal. Remember the Norwegian expedition reached the South Pole on the exact day they had planned (check out the story in Chapter 12).

Maintaining focus is challenging when it comes to staying the course on a long-term goal or even staying in a place of concentration during our daily tasks. The long-term focus is easily fixed with structure. Creating, documenting, and frequently communicating the vision and mission will nurture a collective understanding and concentration on reaching it.

When it comes to staying focused in the present moment, Right Concentration has become significantly more challenging through the overwhelming amount of technology that constantly distracts us. The misconception that multitasking improves productivity has been disproven time and time again. Research by the American Psychological Association shows that taking on more than one task at a time reduces productivity and cognitive performance. There is a time cost to the mental juggling of switching that also results in a decreased ability to accomplish complex tasks or problem-solve.

Stop starting and start finishing. Prioritize the most important things to be done each day, and do them first thing in the morning. Mark Twain once said, "Eat a live frog first thing in the morning, and nothing worse will happen to you the rest of the day." What he means is, do the hardest task first rather than putting it off. Our best time to do complex work is early in our day—ideally, not long after you wake up in the morning. The worst strategy is to do all the small and simple tasks first. Yes, you do get an easy win, but that takes up the ideal time mentally to do the hard work, and it's wasted on the simple and quick tasks that can be done at the end of the day. Prioritize the most important work and start with that. Don't stop until it's complete, then move to the next item on your list after a short break to move your body or meditate as an active recovery.

Moving our body to recover might seem counterintuitive, but most of us do our "work" sitting in a chair staring at a computer screen. Active recovery through movement increases the flow of blood to your muscles and brain, helping energize your body while mentally recovering.

Mindfulness is a recovery superpower. Meditation studies have shown that it impacts two parts of our brain: our attention and our emotions. These studies have found that even just two weeks of meditation, 30 minutes per day, shows a different pattern of brain activity. When we combine an active recovery movement like walking, swimming, or yoga with a mediation practice, it creates the ideal mental and physical state not only to perform at our peak, but also to help us live in our best possible state of mental health.

Tool: Black and White Rocks for Keeping Score

Buddhist monks use a technique to help them have the right thoughts. They carry a small bag with black and white stones in their pocket. Anytime they have a positive thought, they place a single white stone in a pouch. If they have a negative thought, they place a black stone in the pouch. At the end of the day, the monk pours out his stones to reveal how many positive and how many negative thoughts he has had throughout the day.

Try this for one week, whether it's white or black stones, nickels and pennies, or anything else to track your positive thoughts and negative impressions. Keep track and see how monitoring it impacts your behavior and thoughts.

What is the ratio of positive thoughts (white rocks) to negative thoughts (black rocks) today?

_____

_____

_____

List the positive thoughts that you remember.

_____

_____

_____

(continued)

(*continued*)

_____

_____

_____

List the negative thoughts that you remember.

_____

_____

_____

_____

_____

_____

The Enlightened Entrepreneur

Let me start by clarifying that I do not claim to be an enlightened entrepreneur. I am grateful to have found my path and continue to work on following the road less traveled. Maybe the title for this chapter could be "The Awakened Entrepreneur," but I don't want the concept of enlightenment to feel impossible to achieve. It is already within all of us.

When you start to walk the path that feels right in your heart, the journey has begun. Finding our purpose is not something that happens quickly for most of us, but I promise you it's worth the effort. Life is a precious gift that is meant to be lived in pursuit of reaching our full potential in the short time we have on earth.

The healthiest approach is to accept failure as a possibility in the beginning and then move forward once we have acknowledged that potential. This acceptance of the challenges and setbacks that are inevitable allows us to continue without fear or hesitation. When you recognize the outcomes that are not in alignment with your vision, it allows you to accept and move past them, but it also helps identify the challenges that are possible to triumph over and proactively work to overcome them.

Karma in Business and Life

We can't have a book about the Zen of business and not address how Karma impacts our personal and professional lives. Always act in a way that does not create negative Karma. Buddhists believe that our actions have an impact on our lives and our future lives. In Sanskrit, Karma simply means "action." The theory of Karma is fundamental to Buddhist belief and is understood as a literal manifestation of the law of cause and effect. Buddhist Karma refers to actions driven by intention (*cetanā*) through body, speech, or mind. It is the idea that intentional actions have consequences in future lives. These can be physical, verbal, or even mental actions. Right Concentration (see Chapter 22) is the root of our Karma.

In this world, nothing happens to a person that they do not deserve for some reason. These are the results of our past actions. Karma is a law of nature, so actions are followed by consequences, not as a result of divine judgment but instead natural law—the law of cause and effect.

Karma Defined

Karma is intentional action. Based on the intention, Karma can be divided into two separate paths, wholesome actions or unwholesome actions:

- **Kusala Karma:** Wholesome actions with positive results in this life or the next or in terms of enlightenment. Kusala Karma comes from non-greed, non-hate, and non-delusion.

- **Akusala Karma:** Unwholesome actions with negative results in this life or the next or in terms of enlightenment. Akusala Karma comes from greed, hate, and delusion.

When we plant a seed, it has the potential to generate a series of experiences in the future. Karma (intentional action) comes in three forms: Actions of the Mind, Actions of Speech, and Actions of the Body.

- **Actions of the Mind:** Anger, greed, jealousy, and general negative thoughts are Actions of the Mind related to your Karma. This means fostering negativity in your mind can impact your Karma in the same way as Actions of Speech or Actions of the Body.
- **Actions of Speech:** Lying, abusive, or hateful speech and spreading rumors are Actions of Speech. My personal rule is that I will not say or put in writing anything about a person that I would not say in their presence.
- **Actions of the Body:** Harming others, unethical sexual activity, and stealing are examples of Actions of the Body that create negative Karma.

The key to remember in all three forms of Karma is the intention behind the action.

Karma at Work

One of the five core values at my agency was "Perpetual Karma." That meant we took the same approach to business relationships and interactions that I applied to my personal life. Everyone who was employed at the agency was measured quarterly in terms of how they embodied the core values. It mattered to me, as well as to my staff, that we always did right by our clients.

Karma doesn't work like a savings account. You don't do a good deed expecting to receive immediate return on investment (ROI). Working at a homeless shelter this week doesn't mean closing that new dream client the following week. Karma is not something you can keep score of, because it spans all of our lives.

A true judge of someone's character is how they treat someone who can do nothing for them.

The Three Mountains

In our lifetime, we have three mountains to climb. The first mountain is in service of ourselves—building our business or climbing the corporate ladder of financial success and recognition. Most people never make it to the summit of the first mountain. They spend their lives craving more than they currently have, turning this mountain into a never-ending treadmill. This mountain, sadly for most, is the only peak they will attempt to climb, completely unaware of the existence of the second and third.

Of the few who do reach the summit of the first mountain, only some see the second mountain in the distance. Climbing this mountain is in service of others. How can you help someone else live their best life? A rare few actually see the second mountain while climbing the first and find a way to go straight to summiting the mountain that serves others. It is not required to reach the summit of the first mountain before beginning your trek up the second.

Off in the far distance is the third mountain. To take on climbing this mountain is to be in service of the entire world. The best example of this is Norman Borlaug, an American agronomist who developed high-yielding, disease-resisting wheat varieties with broad adaptation to various growing conditions. Rather than make a fortune off his work, Norman moved to Mexico and did manual labor in the wheat fields, saving a million people from starvation in Mexico. Afterward, he moved his family to India, where he multiplied the region's grain output fourfold. These new wheat varieties and crop management transformed agricultural production, creating what is known today as the "Green Revolution." When he finally returned home, he worked on farms all over China and Africa. Norman prevented over a billion men, women, and children from dying of starvation. In his work to prevent hunger and famine around the world, it is said that Dr. Borlaug has "saved more lives than any one person in human history."

What can you do to make the world a better place? What transformational impact on humanity is your Ikigai? (See Chapter 16 for more on Ikigai.) If you don't think you can change the world, I believe you are wrong. What if you have an impact on one person? It could be an employee or a random person walking down the street. Remember the note left by the man who jumped to his death from the Golden Gate Bridge? The note he left said that he would not jump if just one person had smiled at him that day. If you don't think that helping a single person could change the world, imagine that person being the one who created the cure for cancer.

In Conclusion

What initially attracted me to Buddhism was the Middle Way. The concept was that reaching nirvana didn't require perfection but rather moderation. As I dove deeper into Buddhist teachings, it was obvious how these ideas applied to modern business applications.

Right Understanding creates a foundation that we can use as our North Star. It is indeed our compass, and it informs everything we think, say, and do. Right Thought is our clarity of vision, and our thoughts constantly plant seeds that will grow through our speech and actions. Right Speech is understanding how important our words are and that how we listen must be mastered to be effective. Inspiring leaders are better than those who try to motivate only through incentivizing.

Right Action is how we act every day. Our actions should bring no harm to ourselves or others while contributing to the world in a positive way. Right Livelihood is how we earn a living. When we can find our Ikigai, aligning our reason for living with our livelihood, there is no line between what we do for joy and what we do for work.

Right Mindfulness teaches us the importance of meditation, modern research shows the scientific benefits of this ancient practice, and Right Concentration helps being present and with focus.

Today is a gift; tomorrow is not guaranteed for any of us. Use your time wisely today and spend it as if it was your last day on earth.

In the end, only three things matter: how much you loved, how gently you lived, and how gracefully you let go of things not meant for you.
                                                                    —Buddha

---

Tool: The Four Sevens

Imagine that you just left your doctor's office. I want you to imagine that it was not a good visit; in fact, you received some horrible news. Your doctor told you that seven years from today would be the last day of this life. With that burden of knowledge, write down everything you still want to accomplish in this life.

Seven years: _____

_____

_____

_____

_____

_____

_____

_____

Now imagine the same doctor's visit, but it was much
worse news. Your doctor told you that you have
seven months to live—barely over half a year. Describe
how you would spend those seven months.

Seven months: _____

_____

_____

_____

_____

_____

Same doctor's visit but even more tragic news. Instead
of seven months, you are given seven short weeks to live.
With less than two months left in this life, how will you
spend those final seven weeks?

Seven weeks: _____

_____

_____

_____

_____

_____

_____

(continued)

(*continued*)

This time it's the worst possible scenario. Your doctor gave you one week to live. How would you spend each previous day if you knew it was your last week on earth?

Seven days: _____

_____

_____

_____

_____

_____

_____

_____

This exercise is meant to help you find clarity into what really matters in your life. Most of us neglect the most important parts of our lives (family, partner, friends, experiences, etc.) while we pursue a future that might never arrive. By understanding what truly matters in life, we can focus our time and energy on where it truly matters.

Acknowledgments

Rich and Rob. My mom and dad. Mindy. All of my forum mates and EO friends.

About the Author

Keith Roberts is an entrepreneur, author, and keynote speaker. He started Zenman in 1998, creating brands and building websites for some of the most prominent brands in the world. In 2015 Keith created a sister agency called Bigfoot Web to serve a broader customer base. After two decades of running the agency, Keith had a moment of clarity that he was trading his time for money and made the conscious decision to find his Ikigai. That led him to creating the OAK Journal and embarking on a journey that took him to five continents on his path. In 2020, Keith sold Zenman, making a conscious shift to following his life's purpose.

Index

3-2-1-Zero email, 105–106
10-10-10 Morning Routine, 144
16 Personalities test, 28

A

Acceptance, challenge, 84
Actions, 33
    core belief, equivalence, 47–49
    daily actions, focus, 137
    daily goodness, tool, 161–162
    importance, 138
    kindness, usage, 94
    priorities, alignment, 140–141
    purposefulness, 136–137
Actions of Speech, 221
Actions of the Body, 221
Actions of the Mind, 221
Active recovery (Flow State Routine
        component), 145
Adrenaline, release, 86
Adventure, core value, 178
Agile methodology, 86
Akusala karma, 221
Alertness, 154–155
Amundsen, Roald, 139
Anatta, practice, 76
Anicca, practice, 76
Anxiety, future (relationship),
        102
AOL, visitation amount, 7

Apple (company vision), 173
Arguments, winning desire
        (release), 14
Arrogance (self-sabotaging
        behavior), 43
Arrows, impact, 214
Attraction, law. See Law of
        Attraction
Audience, understanding, 126
Awards, receiving (identification), 27
Awareness (Sati), 101
    acquisition, 75–76
    subconscious awareness, 95

B

Backlog, retention, 71
Balance
    creation, tool, 189
    finding, 158–159
Bates, Edward, 15
Beginner's mind. See Shoshin
Being present (Sati), 101
Best-case scenarios, 215
Bezos, Jeff, 51
Big Hairy Audacious Goal (BHAG),
        95, 174
    understanding, 26
    writing, 210
Binge shopping (self-sabotaging
        behavior), 43

Black and White Rocks (tool),
    217–218
BlackBerry, disappearance, 77
Blockbuster, disappearance, 77
Blood pressure, reduction, 154
Body
    language, awareness, 117
    Six Pairs of Sense Basis
        components, 201
        actions, 221
Boeree, C. George, 201
Borlaug, Norman, 222–223
Box breathing, usage, 148–149
Brin, Sergey, 4
Brooks Institute, differentiation,
        185–186
Bryant, Kobe, 41
Buddhism, foundation, 17
Business
    actions, importance, 138
    challenges, 86
    communication
        challenges, 124–128
        tools, defining, 130–132
    core values, determina-
        tion, 175–178
    discipline, clarity (requirement),
        67, 68–71
    Dukkha, usage, 21–31
    ideas, 127
    impermanence, usage, 76–77
    karma, usage, 220
    Law of Attraction, usage, 210–211
    Magga, impact, 33
    mindfulness, benefits, 107
    Nirodha, impact, 32
    objectives, achievement, 95
    personal core values, alignment,
        159–160
    real estate ownership, 27
    Right Action, usage, 137–139
    Right Concentration,
        usage, 215–217
    Right Effort, usage, 185–187

Right Livelihood, usage,
    159–160
Right Mindfulness, usage,
    203–204
Right Speech, usage, 117–118
Right Understanding, usage,
    64–71
Samudāya, impact, 31–32
Sati usage, 107–108
scaling, consequences, 22
spiritual, combination, 6–9
success, usage, 160–161
types, avoidance, 158
vision, clarity (requirement),
    67–68
Wabi-sabi, usage, 86–87
warrior monk, actions, 146–149
WHY statement, 173
Zen, 134

C
Calmness, 154–155
Camping, activity (usage),
    154–155
Capabilities, identification, 163
Capacity, cultivation, 168–169
Cartrey, Jim, 208–209
Cash flow
    Dukkha, relationship, 21–23
    issues, experience, 22
    sales, absence (impact), 22
Cause of suffering (Four Noble
        Truths component), 201
Cavafy, C.P., 95
Chase, Salmon P., 15
Cholesterol, reduction, 154
Circulation, improvement, 154
Citta (mindfulness foundation),
    200, 201
Clarity, 57
    absence, categories, 124–126
    importance, 26–28
    leadership issues, impact,
        124–125

one-on-one communications,
    quality problem, 124–126
Clients
    attraction, 23–26
    Dukkha, relationship, 23–27
    opportunity, treatment
        (benefits), 24
    suffering, 23
Cognitive performance
    improvement, 107
    reduction, 216
Collaboration, fostering
        (absence), 127
Collective performance, 29
Communication
    art, Zen (relationship), 123
    breakdowns/challenges,
        123–124, 125
    business communication,
        challenges, 124–128
    channels
        confusion, 124, 128–129
        tool, 130
    intention, determination,
        125–126
    nonverbal communication, 117
        mastery, 118
    one-on-one communications,
        quality problem, 124,
        125–126
Company
    awards/patents, receiving
        (identification), 27
    Big Hairy Audacious Goal
        (BHAG), understanding, 26
    employees, number
        (determination), 27
    goals, creation/declaration, 26
    town hall (business
        communication tool), 131–132
    vision, 173
        identification, 97
        short-term objectives,
            alignment, 137

Concentration (Seven Factors
        of Enlightenment
        component), 33, 201
Confidence, absence, 44
Consciousness (Five Aggregate
        component), 201
Consistency
    appearance, 136f
    importance, 137
    indispensability, 186–187
Continuation Ceremony, 9
Control, illusion, 77
Conversations, break, 115
Coping mechanisms,
        development, 42
Core belief, thoughts/actions
        (equivalence), 47–49
Core hours, Zenman technique, 69
Core values
    business core values,
        determination, 175–178
    hire alignment question, 30–31
    identification, 176
    importance, 174
    personal core values,
        determination, 178
    Process Gurus, 176–177
    reinforcement, 125
    standard operating procedures
        (SOPs), contrast, 174
    test, 30–31
    tool, 179–180
    types, 177
Cortisol
    reduction, 152
    release, 85–86
Cost of goods sold (COGS), 23
Covid pandemic (illusion,
        control), 77
Creative work, delivery
        (consistency), 25
Creativity
    blocking, 83
    core value, 178

Creativity (*continued*)
  downtime, need, 104
  enhancement, 107
Credibility, establishment, 24
Customer relationship
    management (CRM),
    nonusage (reasons), 129
Customers
  commitment, reputation
      increase, 24
  project case studies, creation, 24

D
Daily actions, focus, 137
Daily goodness, action
    (tool), 161–162
Daily practices, 144–145
Daily Progress, importance, 139
Dalai Lama, Lopsang interaction, 5
Day-to-day life, presence (practice
    tool), 108–109
Deadlines, missing (self-sabotaging
    behavior), 43
Death, avoidance, 193
Decision-making, 29
  tool, 174
Declaration of Independence, 41
Deep work, execution, 69
Dependability, indispensability,
    186–187
Depression, 168
  past, relationship, 102
Desire (poison), 20
  harm, 67
Devices, blue light (emission), 104
Dhamma (mindfulness foundation),
    200, 201
Diet, impact, 209
Discipline, 188
  clarity, requirement, 67, 68–71
  impact, 147
  improvement, tools, 68–71
Discontentment, fostering, 102–103
DISC test, 28

Disengagement, impact, 124, 128
Distraction, avoidance/elimination,
    69, 204
Donaldson, Jimmy, 32
Doubt (Five Hindrance
    component), 201
Downtime, need, 104
Drive (Pink), 160
Due diligence, 29
Duke, Annie, 65–66
Dukkha (problem) (noble truth
    component), 18
  business usage, 21–31
  suffering, truth, 18–20

E
Ear (Six Pairs of Sense Basis
    components), 201
Early warning sign, 43
Earnings before interest, taxes,
    depreciation, and
    amortization (EBITDA),
    determination, 26
Edison, Thomas, 103, 137
Ego
  clearance, 57–58
  release, tool, 88–89
Emerging technologies,
    investment, 77
Emotions, identification attempt,
    92
Employees
  happiness, increase, 107
  mindfulness practice, 108
Endearing speech, usage, 129
Energy (Seven Factors of Enlighten-
    ment component), 201
Energy, focus, 213–214
Enlightenment, 147
  Seven Factors (mindfulness
      group), 201
Enneagram test, 28
Entrepreneur, enlightenment, 219
Entrepreneurship, finding, 2–4

Entrepreneurs' Organization (EO),
    joining, 127
Environment (safety), absence
    (impact), 124, 127
Equanimity (Seven Factors of
    Enlightenment component),
    201
Evening routine, 109
Evil talk, absence, 115–116
Excellence, delivery, 24
Expense levels, payment reasons,
    25
Experience, involvement process
    (determination), 125, 126
Extraneous communication,
    removal, 106
Eye (Six Pairs of Sense Basis
    components), 201

F
Failure
    acceptance, 219–220
    fear, root cause, 45
    frequency, 193–194
    learning/iteration method, 64
Family, focus, 133–134
Fatherhood, core value, 178
Feed the Children, vision, 174
Feeling (Five Aggregate
    component), 201
Fight or flight responses, 85–86
Financial neglect (self-sabotaging
    behavior), 43
Fire-ready-aim approach, 187
Five Aggregates (mindfulness
    group), 201
Five Hindrances (mindfulness
    group), 201
Flow Research Collective,
    studies, 69–70
Flow State Routine, components,
    145
Flow state, usage, 68–70
Focus areas, identification, 189

Focused work (Flow State Routine
    component), 145
Focus, maintenance, 215
Forecasting, accuracy, 21
Forest bathing (Shinrin
    Yoku), 85, 151
    monthly Shinrin Yoku, usage, 156
    nature, experiencing, 156
    practice, 153, 154
    tool, 155–156
    weekly Shinrin Yoku,
        usage, 155–156
Form (Five Aggregate
    component), 201
Formations (Five Aggregate
    component), 201
Four Noble Truths, 17, 47
    mindfulness group, 201
    summarization, 18–21
Four Sevens (tool), 224–226
Four Signs, 18
Franklin, Benjamin, 161
Frost, Robert, 3
Fulfillment (Ikigai element),
    165, 167
Future
    shaping, habits (usage), 138
    visualization, tool, 33–37, 208
Future press release (tool), 98–99

G
Gamma brain waves, impact, 202
Gates, Bill, 51, 85
Gautama, Siddhartha, 18
Global pandemic, control
    (absence), 22
Goals
    achievement, 58
    achievement, factors, 209
    observation, 214
    setting, 67, 210
    statement, 97
Goodwill, cultivation, 92, 93–94
Gossip, absence, 115–116

Gratitude (Ikigai element), 166–167
Great Recession, losses, 22
Greed (poison), 20
"Green Revolution," 223

H
Habits
    impact, 209
    latent habits, 42
    negative habits, 143–144
    usage, 138
Hanh, Thich Nhat, 57, 123
Happiness, 169–170
    appearance, 94
    pursuit, 41
Hardship, manifestation, 95
Harm, avoidance, 158–159
Hatred (poison), 20
Headcount, reduction (option), 22
Health, 40
    neglect, self-sabotaging
        behavior, 43
Heart strength, improvement,
    154
Heraclitus, 76
Hires
    examination, 28
    job capability, 29–30
    job fitness, ability, 28–29
    vision/core values, alignment
        question, 30–31
Hoffman, Jeff, 160–161
Honnold, Alex, 68
Human face-to-face interaction,
    removal, 124
Humiliation, suffering
    (avoidance), 105
Huynh, Kym, 138–139

I
"I Am" mantras (tool), 211–212
Ibotta, app design (Right
        Understanding case
        study), 66

Ignorance
    meditation, absence (impact),
        204
    poison, 20
Ikigai (Reason for Living), 163
    capacity, cultivation, 168–169
    elements, 164–167
    finding, 42, 167–168
        tool, 170–172
    gratitude, 166–167
    initiation, 7
    magic, 165–167
    motivation, 166
    purpose/fulfillment, 165
    self-control, 166
    self-realization, 167
    Venn diagram, 163–164, 164f
    Western interpretation, 163, 164f
Ill-will (Five Hindrance
        component), 201
Imperfect, beauty (finding), 83
Imperfection, acceptance (Wabi-sabi
        principle), 84–85
    tool, 88–89
Impermanence (Annica), 75, 214
    business usage, 76–77
    embracing, 78–79
Imposter syndrome (root cause), 45
Improvements, focus, 184
indulgence/self-denial extremes,
        middle way (Buddha), 21
Industry Innovators, 177, 178
Inner monk, embracing, 143
Inner strength, origin, 146–147
Innovation, downtime (need), 104
In-person interactions, 124
Intentional misrepresentation,
        impact, 124, 129
Intentions
    determination, 125–126
    setting, 209
Investigation (Seven Factors of
        Enlightenment
        component), 201

In vino veritas, phrase
        (translation), 114
Izanagi/Izanami, tale, 192

J
Jobs, Steve, 3, 51, 64, 85, 203
    visualization, usage, 96
Jordan, Michael, 146
Journaling, 10-10-10 Morning
        Routine component, 144
"Jumpers" (*New Yorker* article),
        115

K
Kaizen, concept, 184
Kanban (system), 71
Karma (intentional action)
    defining, 220–221
    forms, 221
    harm, 67
    types, 220–221
    usage, 220, 221–222
Kāyā (mindfulness foundation),
        200
Key performance indicators
        (KPIs), 129
    creation, 27
    tracking, 126
Kindness
    power, 115–116
    usage, 94
Kusala karma, 220
Kwik, Jimmy, 45–46

L
Latent habits, 42
Laughter, core value, 178
Law of Attraction, 95, 207
    business usage, 210–211
    embracing, 208–210
Leadership
    core values, 178
    issues, impact, 124–125
Leaders, praise, 117

Lean Product Development,
        approach, 86
Letters, life impact (tool), 119–121
Lies, absence, 115–116
Life
    balance, 76
    change, letter usage
        (tool), 119–121
    karma, usage, 220
    purpose, possession, 170
Life is suffering (Four Noble Truths
        component), 201
Lion Tracker's Guide to Life
        (Varty), 103
Listening, increase, 14–15
Litchell, Dave, 186
Livelihood, 33
    professions, avoidance, 56
Living, deliberateness, 155
Longevity, 169–170
Loves, identification, 164
Lovett, Ron, 125

M
Magga (suffering cessation path)
        (noble truth component),
        18, 51
    business usage, 33
    path, truth, 21
Mantra, usage, 214
May, Jimmy, 193
Meditation (Zen), 143
    10-10-10 Morning Routine
        component, 144
    absence, 204
    embracing, hesitation, 146
    magic, 202–203
    reasons, 146, 204
    studies, 216–217
    tool, 205
    usage, 200–203
Middle Path
    following, 157
    necessity, 72

Middle Way (Noble Eightfold path), 21, 33, 187, 209
 discovery, 44–47
 finding, core techniques, 46
 sections, 33
Mind
 actions, 221
 Effort/Mindfulness/Concentration, 33
 inner chatter, clearance, 57–58
 parachute, comparison, 14
 samadhi, 181
 usage/impact, 94
Mind (Six Pairs of Sense Basis components), 201
Mindfulness, 33. *See also* Right Mindfulness
 achievement, meditation (usage), 200–203
 benefits, 107
 Citta, 200, 201
 Dhamma, 200, 201
 embracing, 204
 employee practice, 108
 foundations, 200–201
 groups, 201
 Kāyā, 200
 practice, 200
  Middle Way discovery technique, 46
 recovery superpower, 216–217
 Sati, 101
 Seven Factors of Enlightenment component, 201
 training efforts, 102
 Vedanā, 200
Minimal viable product (MVP) approach, usage, 68, 70–71, 84–85
 building, 87
Minor improvements, focus, 184
Misogi, 191
 history, 192–193
 roadmap, tool, 195–197
 rules, 193–195
Mission, 173
 communication, 215
 defining, 175
 strategic missions, short-term objectives, 173
Momentum, creation (tool), 189
Money, losses, 22
Moral business, success, 55
Morale, improvement, 107
Morality (sila), 33, 111
Morality (Speech/Action/Livelihood), 33
Morning routine, 109
Motivation
 Ikigai element, 166
 impact, 67
 increase, 204
Mountains, climbing, 222–223
Myers-Briggs test, 28
Mystical fox/butterfly, fable, 134–136

N
Nachi Waterfall, 192
Nature
 connection (Wabi-sabi principle), 85–86
 experiencing, 156
Negative habits, 143–144
Negative patterns
 recognition, 94
 release, 92
Negative self-talk (self-sabotaging behavior), 43
Negative thoughts, release, 92, 93
Neurotransmitters, evolution, 85–86
Nirodha (remedy realization) (noble truth), 18
 business usage, 32
 suffering, cessation (truth), 20

Nirvana, path, 5–6
Noble Eightfold path (Middle Way), 21, 33, 51, 188
  discovery, 44–47
  finding, core techniques, 46
  sections, 33
Noble Silence, practice, 54
Noble Truths. *See* Four Noble Truths
Noise pollution, impact, 152
Nonattachment (Anatta/Anicca), practice, 76
Nonself (Anatta), 76
Nonverbal communication, 117
  mastery, 118
Nose (Six Pairs of Sense Basis components), 201

O
OAK Journal, 8
Obesity, epidemic, 137
Objectives, SMART goals dissection, 27
On-demand expectation, 101–102
One-on-one communications, quality problem, 124, 125–126
One-on-one meetings (business communication tool), 130–131
Operations, state/country expansion (identification), 27
Organization
  decimation, factors, 22
  scaling, 123–124
  suffering, creation, 24
Outcome
  determination, 125, 126
  manifestation, 137–138
  visualization, 208–209
Output, increase, 107
Overnight success, myth, 66

P
Page, Larry, 4
Parkinson's Law, concept, 106
Passive recovery, 145
Past
  dreaming, 103
  release, 102–103
Patents, receiving (identification), 27
Path
  brightening, 133
  finding, 4–6, 39, 204
    Unalone (enlightenment path), 40–41, 41f
Path to end suffering (Four Noble Truths component), 201
Patience, practice, 147
Payment, determination, 163
Peace, present (relationship), 102
Perceptions (Five Aggregate component), 201
Perfectionism (self-sabotaging behavior), 43
Perpetual Karma, 177–178
  value, 177–178
Personal challenges, 86
Personal core values
  business, alignment, 159–160
Personal life, karma (impact), 221–222
Person, name (remembering), 116
Phones, disengagement (result), 104–105
Physical/mental health, damage, 143–144
Picasso, Pablo, 67
Pink, Daniel, 160
Pivotal Labs, interview process, 29
Planning (Flow State Routine component), 145
Poision. *See* Three Poisons

Positive affirmations, practice (Middle Way discovery technique), 46
Positive habits, development (Middle Way discovery technique), 46
Post-traumatic stress disorder (PTSD), 202
veterans assistance, 200
Potential hires, categories, 28–31
Presence, practice tool, 108–109
Priorities/actions, alignment tool, 140–141
Priority task, 146
Problem-solving, need (release), 15
Process-driven characteristic, 25
Process Gurus (core value), 176–177
Procrastination (self-sabotaging behavior), 43
initiation, 43–44
Product
exceptional value, 157
quality, customer examination, 24
Productivity, reduction, 216
Project case studies, creation, 24
Purpose (Ikigai element), 165

Q
Quantitative Creativity, 177
Quarterly initiative, writing, 210
Quarterly Sales Quota, 97

R
Rapture (Seven Factors of Enlightenment component), 201
Reading, 10-10-10 Morning Routine component, 144
Real estate, ownership, 27
Reality, experience, 53
Reason for Living. *See* Ikigai
Recovery superpower, 216–217
Relationships, focus, 133–134
Religion, devotion, 2

Reputation Guardians, 177, 178
Restlessness (Five Hindrance component), 201
Resulting bias, 65
Results, tool, 205
Return on investment (ROI), obtaining, 166–167, 222
Revenue, determination, 26
Reward-based model, 160
RFP process, 79
Right Action (Samma kammanta) (Noble Eightfold path component), 33, 52, 55, 133
business usage, 137–139
Daily Progress, importance, 139
Two-Minute Rule, 139
Right Concentration (Samma samadhi) (Noble Eightfold path component), 33, 52, 57–58, 213
business usage, 215–217
practice, 58
Right decisions, determination (possibility), 65
Right Effort (Samma vayama) (Noble Eightfold path component), 33, 52, 56–57, 183
aspects, 56–57
business usage, 185–187
consistency, 188
principles, 183–185
Right Livelihood (Samma ajiva) (Noble Eightfold path component), 33, 52, 55–56, 157
balance, finding, 158–159
business usage, 159–160
harm, avoidance, 158–159
Right Mindfulness (Samma sati) (Noble Eightfold path component), 33, 52, 57, 199, 203–204

Right Speech (Samma vaca) (Noble Eightfold path component), 14, 33, 52, 54–55, 113
  business usage, 117–118
  principles, 113–117
  timing, 114–115
  tools, 113, 116–117
  workplace cultivation, 118–119
Right Thought (Samma sankappa) (Noble Eightfold path component), 33, 52, 53–54, 91
  business usage, 94–97
  goodwill, cultivation, 92, 93–94
  negative thoughts/patterns, release, 92, 93
  practice, 94
  stages, 92–94
  state, creation, 101
  thought process, aware-ness, 92–93
  usage, 97
Right Understanding (Samma ditthi) (Noble Eightfold path component), 33, 52–53, 63
  business usage, 64–71
  case study, 66
  practice, method, 72
  Right View, 63
  teachings, 84
Risk, minimization, 70
"Road Less Traveled, The" (Frost), 3
Rob's Pair Interview (RPI), 29
Root causes, components, 45
Routines, creation (tool), 149–150

S
Safe environment, creation, 118–119
Sales, absence (impact), 22
Samadhi. *See* Mind
Sampanjañña (clear comprehension), 101

Samudāya (cause) (noble truth component), 18, 63
  business usage, 31–32
  suffering, cause (truth), 20
Sati (awareness/mindfulness). *See* Being present
  business usage, 107–108
Scaling, money (need), 22
Scared money, result, 4
Seinfeld, Jerry, 203
Self-awareness, presence, 43–44
Self-care, practice, 147–149
Self-cherishing, 147–148
Self-comparison, trap, 184
Self-control
  discipline, impact, 147
  Ikigai element, 166
Self-deprivation, impact, 5–6
Self-esteem, low level (root cause), 45
Self-medication (self-sabotaging behavior), 43
Self-realization (Ikigai element), 167
Self-sabotage
  addressing, 42–44
  behaviors, examples, 43
  seeds, 45–46
  usage, 45
Sense Bases, Six Pairs (mindfulness group), 201
Sensual desire (Five Hindrance component), 201
Service, exceptional value, 157
Seven Factors of Enlightenment (mindfulness group), 201
Seward, William H., 15
Sexual intimacy, 55
Shaolin monks, characteristics, 146–147
Shaolin philosophy, characteristics, 147
Shaolin practice, principles, 147–149
Shared vision, possession, 174

Shinrin Yoku. *See* Forest bathing
Shinto tradition, 191
Short-term missions, 175
Short-term objectives, strategic
        missions (alignment), 173
Shoshin (beginner's mind), 13
Simple, measurable, attainable,
        relevant, and timebound
        (SMART) goals,
        identification, 27
Sinek, Simon, 169
Six Pairs of Sense Bases
        (mindfulness group), 201
Slack, usage, 129
Sleep, pharmaceuticals (avoidance),
        148–149
Sloth (Five Hindrance component),
        201
Small businesses, bootstrapping,
        78
Socrates, 15
Software development
        methodology, 86
Speaking
    decrease, 14–15
    intentionality, 210
    kindness, usage, 94
Speech
    actions, 221
    advantages, 129
Standard operating procedures
        (SOPs)
    core values, contrast, 174
    creation, 176
Standing still, fear, 138
Stanton, Edwin, 15
Statement, creation, 174–175
Stern, Howard, 2023
Stop and Start list (tool), 58
Stop starting, start finishing
        (discipline tool), 68, 71
Strategic missions, short-term
        objectives, 173

Strategic partner, development,
        78–79
Stress
    coping mechanisms,
        development, 42
    feeling, 143–144
    hormone, impact, 152
    reduction, 107
String theory, quantum mechanics
        (merger), 95
Subconscious acts, creation, 44–45
Subconscious awareness, 95
Success, reaching, 2–3
Suffering
    aspects (Buddha), 19
    cause/cessation/path (Four Noble
        Truths component), 201
    cessation, 18, 201
    examples, 19
    forms, 18
    organizations, creation, 24
    truth, 18–20
Sullivan, Dan, 168
Support system, existence (Middle
        Way discovery technique),
        46
Suzuki, Shunryu, 14

T
"Take Ownership" (core value
        test), 30–31
Tanhā, 20
Tasks, multitasking, 216
Team meetings (business
        communication tool),
        131
Team Wikispeed, 86
Technology
    boundary, 109
    distractions, 104–106, 108
    themes, crafting, 176–177
Thinking in Bets (Duke), 64
This, too, shall pass (tool), 80–82

Thoughts, 33
  awareness, 92–93
  benefits, question, 93
  core belief, equivalence, 47–49
  identification, attempt, 92
  kindness, question, 93
  process, consciousness, 93
  wrong thought, example, 96
Three Poisons, 20
Tiger and the Strawberry (Zen
    parable), 106–107
Time (resource, preciousness),
    133–136
Tone, awareness, 117
Tongue (Six Pairs of Sense Basis
    components), 201
Tranquility (Seven Factors of
    Enlightenment component),
    201
Transcendental Meditation
    (TM), 202, 203
  introduction, 203–204
Transience, appreciation (Wabi-sabi
    principle), 85
Transparency, absence (impact),
    124, 127–128
Trauma, 202
  root cause, 45
Triggers, identification/removal
    (Middle Way discovery
    technique), 46
Trusted circle, 209
Truthfulness, inclusion, 55
Truths
  challenging, tool, 72–74
  Four Noble Truths (mindfulness
    group), 201
Two-Minute Rule, 139

U
Uketamo, 87
Unalone (enlightenment path),
    40–41, 41f

Under-promising/overdelivery,
    impact, 24
Understanding, 33
Unsafe environment, impact,
    124, 127
Unwholesome qualities, prevention/
    extinguishment (effort), 56

V
Values, 173
  core values, importance, 174
  definition, 177
Varty, Boyd, 103
Vedanā (mindfulness foun-
    dation), 200
VIDA (Lovett ownership), 159
Vision, 173
  clarification, 174–175
  clarity, requirement, 67–68
  communication, 215
  company vision, identification, 97
  defining, 174–175
  hire alignment question, 30–31
  shared vision, possession, 174
  why, reminding, 210
Visualization
  power, 95–97
  success, 208–209
  work, 91–92
Vocabulary, awareness, 117

W
Wabi-sabi (imperfect/impermanent
    beauty, finding), 83
  business usage, 86–87
  imperfection, acceptance, 84–85
  nature, connection, 85–86
  principles, 84–86
  transience, appreciation, 85
Warrior monk, actions, 146–149
Waste, avoidance, 70
Wholesome qualities, cultivation/
    strengthening, 57

Why
  business statement, 173
  reasons, 168–169
  reminding, 210
  starting, importance, 169
Winfrey, Oprah, 203
Win-win, creation, 126
Wisdom (*panna*), 33, 61
  absence, 53
  meditation, impact, 204
Wisdom (Understanding/
      Thought), 33
Wooden, John, 187
Words
  power, 116
  retraction, impossibility, 55
Work
  block, 145
  continuation, 184–185
  creative work, delivery
      (consistency), 25
  deep work, execution, 69
  focused work (Flow State Routine
      component), 145
  forest bathing (Shinrin Yoku),
      practice, 153
  karma, usage, 221–222
  prioritization, 216
Workaholic, actions justification,
      72
Workplace
  conflict, reduction, 107
  human face-to-face interaction,
      removal, 124

  Right Speech, cultivation,
      118–119
World
  improvement, business success
      (usage), 160–161
  needs, 163
Wozniak, 4
Wrong thought, example, 96

Y
Young, Neil, 153

Z
Zen
  communication, relationship, 123
  meaning, 143
  term, usage, 6
Zen Buddhism, mindfulness
      (practice), 200
Zenman, 168
  agency work, 44, 87
  becoming, 1
  contract, 79
  core hours, practice, 69
  five-star rating, 178
  global leader, 7
  initiation, 158
  possessions, 32
  reputation, 25
  resources, 78–79
  selling, 79
Zen Mind, Beginner's Mind
      (Suzuki), 14
Zuckerberg, Mark, 51